Praise for *A Missionary Mindset*

"If we are living in the midst of a 'missional renaissance' (Reggie McNeal), it's time we learned about one of the major architects of today's 'renaissance.' This book is a gentle and wise introduction to the mind and especially the heart of one of the greatest participant-observers in the history of Christian missions: E. Stanley Jones."

—Leonard Sweet, best-selling author of *From Tablet to Table*, Professor (Drew University, George Fox University, and Tabor College), and founder of preachthestory.com

"The family of E. Stanley Jones is indeed grateful to Douglas Ruffle for his efforts to gather insights (and experiences) of Jones' approach to Christian missions. Ruffle works to capture the unwavering focus of my grandfather, which was on Jesus. Jones bet his life on Christ and affirmed that Jesus is the perfect gift of God to mankind and is the focus of a 'missionary mindset.' The heart of the missionary mindset, as Ruffle so clearly affirms, is Jesus Christ, the incarnation of God in Christ, which provides humanity with the experience of God approachable, God available, God simplified, and God lovable. Thanks be to God."

—Anne Mathews-Younes, EdD, DMin., President, The E. Stanley Jones Foundation

"One of the saints of our Wesleyan tradition is E. Stanley Jones. He was Christ-centered and yet open to people of all faiths and no faith. I am grateful to Doug Ruffle for connecting his life and thought with the essential call to plant new Christian communities in our day."

—Ken Carter, Resident Bishop, Florida Area, The United Methodist Church

"We have long spoken of 'mission field' and now finally we have a beautifully written guidebook on how to apply a 'missionary mindset' to reaching new people in our changing world! Doug Ruffle insightfully captures the E. Stanley Jones that I knew and worked with early in my ministry. Sharing personal stories, real-life narratives, and drawing on the life of one of the greatest missionaries of all time, Doug offers an important gift in our commitment to share the love of Jesus Christ through planting new churches and transforming existing ones to become a more authentic witness to Christ in an increasingly multicultural world."

—Jim Ozier, New Church Development &
Congregational Transformation, North Texas Conference,
The United Methodist Church

"In a post-Christian society, how can one present Christ? In a context where people search for meaning and turn to a variety and range of sources, can the message of Jesus still inspire and transform? *A Missionary Mindset* is a challenging and stimulating book that responds to these questions forthrightly and honestly. By returning to and recapturing the essence of the life and legacy of the great missionary Dr. Stanley Jones and opening his mind and heart to a new generation, Dr. Ruffle's book offers a timely and relevant path to all those who earnestly seek to follow the Great Commission. This is a book which needs to be in the library or Kindle of every clergy person and lay disciple who is eager, willing, and committed to practice and live out their Christian discipleship at the present time."

—Bishop Sudarshana Devadhar, Resident Bishop of
the New England Annual Conference, The United Methodist Church

"This book is about Christian mission. Douglas Ruffle, as a 'former' missionary, understands the critical issues of sharing the 'Kingdom of God'—a Stanley Jones passion—in ways that can be understood on the global scene, a missionary mindset 'untrammeled'! Chapter 8 alone, addressing this Kingdom, is easily worth the price of the book.

"Dr. Ruffle writes with passion and balance about the whole gospel for the whole world. The insights shared here should be studied and understood by missionaries (*obreros fraternales*), both at home and abroad."

—Robert G. Tuttle Jr., PhD, Emeritus Professor of
World Christianity, Asbury Theological Seminary

"This book is required reading for leaders serious about developing cultural competencies to effectively interact with people of diverse backgrounds. Doug Ruffle has shared his personal journey to self-awareness, reflection questions, valuable resources, biblical lessons, the profound wisdom of E. Stanley Jones and others. This book is an essential resource as leaders in The United Methodist Church work to become a more global and inclusive church."

> —Rev. Dr. Varlyna D. Wright, District Superintendent, Capital,
> The United Methodist Church of Greater New Jersey

"*A Missionary Mindset* is a journey in remembering our task as leaders in the church and refocusing on how to carry out the Kingdom work to which we are called."

> —Dr. Jeff Olive, Director of New Church Development,
> Texas Annual Conference of The United Methodist Church,
> www.txcumc.org

"From his own experience as a missionary and pastor, Doug Ruffle calls the church to take on a missionary mindset and boldly present the good news of Jesus Christ to the culture that surrounds us. Whether you are a leader in an existing congregation or are being called by God to be a part of a new faith community, this book will both challenge and bless."

> —Bishop Mark J. Webb, Upper New York Annual Conference
> of The United Methodist Church

"*A Missionary Mindset* is a must read for church leaders today as we wrestle with an ever-changing culture. The missional principles of E. Stanley Jones are woven together to show a way for today's church leaders to move out of their default culture and engage their own mission field right where they are. Prayer, learning, listening, and valuing others are just a few of the principles to be grasped in this book."

> —Matt Poole, Lead Pastor, Glen Mar UMC, Ellicott City, MD

"Through story, scripture, and the witness of those who have gone before us and his own ministry, Dr. Ruffle illumines a path for planting and revitalizing churches in a global context. His book is a rich resource for those seeking more than a to-do list as he invites us to be grounded in our identity as Christians in the making."
—Bishop Minerva G. Carcaño, Los Angeles Area, The UMC

"This book should be required reading for any new church start pastor and their launch team. Pastors and lay leaders of existing congregations should also eagerly embrace the biblically sound and culturally sensitive insight it offers. Dr. Ruffle traverses the gap between theory and practice. Insightfully he guides the reader to connect evangelistic witness and compassionate mission with and to those of a post-Christian worldview. I will personally urge my pastors to buy a copy!"
—Bishop Mike Lowry, Resident Bishop of the Central Texas Conference, The United Methodist Church

"Doug thoughtfully brings Dr. E. Stanley Jones back into conversations with us as we wrestle with effectively sharing the Christian faith today. Doug's own missionary experiences in Argentina are interwoven throughout the book, enriching our understanding and appreciation for developing a missionary mindset in our current local ministry settings. An excellent read for church planters and existing church leaders."
—Rev. Dr. Candace Lewis, Executive Director, Path 1 (New Church Starts at Discipleship Ministries)

Every one of us, lay and clergy, is a missionary, right where we are. In order to reach out to more people, younger people, and more diverse people, we must be articulate in the language of the culture. This book is a great gift to those looking for help in becoming equipped to better serve the mission field close at hand as well as the global mission field. I strongly recommend this book to anyone who is serious about God's mission in the world.
—J. Martin Lee, Director of Congregational Development and Redevelopment, Northern Illinois Conference, The UMC

A MISSIONARY
MINDSET

A MISSIONARY
MINDSET

WHAT CHURCH LEADERS NEED TO KNOW
TO REACH THEIR COMMUNITIES

LESSONS FROM E. STANLEY JONES

DOUGLAS RUFFLE

DISCIPLESHIP
RESOURCES

A MISSIONARY MINDSET
What Church Leaders Need to Know to Reach Their Communities
Lessons from E. Stanley Jones

ISBNs
Print: 978-0-88177-844-1
Mobi: 978-0-88177-846-5
eBook: 978-0-88177-845-8
Audio Edition: 978-0-88177-858-8

Library of Congress Control Number: 2016937547

DR 844

To
Hugo Urcola, and the many other friends and mentors
of the Evangelical Methodist Church of Argentina

CONTENTS

PREFACE

In the summer of 2013, staff of Path 1 (New Church Starts at Discipleship Ministries of The United Methodist Church) along with a selected group of associates from around the United States embarked on an extensive "Road Trip." We visited more than 320 of the new churches that were planted in the previous five years. Through hundreds of conversations with church planters and judicatory leaders of congregational development, we learned about the hopes and heartaches of starting new places for new people and revitalizing existing churches among the people called Methodist in the United States. We learned of innovative "out of the box" church plants as well as traditional strategies that are reaching new people and making disciples of Jesus Christ for the transformation of the world. We celebrate the many ways that annual conferences and districts of the church are finding ways to form new communities of faith. We also learned that there was a lack of written resources available that guided new church planting in a Wesleyan theological perspective. As a result, we set out to create *Wesleyan Church Planting Resources*. Our hope is that these resources will not only help those who plant new churches but also help in the revitalization of existing churches.

A Missionary Mindset is part of this initiative. Drawing from my experience as a missionary in Argentina as well as a pastor of local churches and a judicatory director of congregational development, this book is designed to help church leaders navigate the waters of church life in the twenty-first century. It draws upon the wisdom and best practices of missionaries E. Stanley Jones and Roland Allen and offers guidance for church leaders—both clergy and lay—on how to reach their communities. A study guide is offered to help lead a discussion of the issues highlighted. Our prayer is that this resource along with the others in the series will help new church starts and existing churches in their ministry to make disciples of Jesus Christ for the transformation of the world.

I am blessed to work with a great team of people at Path 1 (New Church Starts at Discipleship Ministries) who are supportive in every possible way. The Reverend Dr. Candace Lewis, our executive director, has encouraged me in every step of writing of this book. I owe her a debt of thanks. I received valuable help on the manuscript itself from Philip Brooks, our communications specialist. Pax Escobar, Vivian Rucker, and Alma Perez provided encouragement, support, and patience through the days and weeks this project was under way. Joey Crowe, manager of Discipleship Resources, provided excellent guidance through the steps of publication.

I am indebted to my friend Dr. Young Ho Chun for his insightful conversation when I first mentioned the idea for this book. Dr. Chun introduced me to the notion that we all have a "default culture." Dr. Anne Mathews-Younes, E. Stanley Jones's granddaughter, provided encouragement from the outset and has introduced me to other writers who have a love and respect for her grandfather's writing. She also corrected key information in her grandfather's story. Tom Albin, dean of the Upper Room, gave me several opportunities to speak before the Board of United Christian Ashrams. At one of their meetings, I received very helpful feedback from the group for an early version of chapter 1. I am grateful for the comments and suggestions given by Dr. David

Lowes Watson, who read a rough draft of the manuscript. He helped me see how important it is to articulate clearly just what the gospel is for our readers today. Dr. Stephen Bryant, Director of Discipleship Resources International, also gave insightful help in articulating the essentials of the gospel. I am grateful to friends in Argentina who helped jog my memory of events I experienced while living there. I am especially grateful to Hugo Urcola, Daniel Bruno, and Juan Gattinoni for their help. Beth Gaede provided extraordinarily fine editorial guidance throughout the development of this book. Her coaching and direction have helped clarify my thinking and writing. To these great colleagues I owe deep gratitude. If there is anything worthy in this book, it is because of their help.

In many ways the writing of this book has been a team effort. I am grateful to Path 1 team members William Chaney, Curtis Brown, Paul Nixon, Bob Crossman, and Sam Rodriguez for their helpful suggestions. A circle of readers read a first draft of the book and gave me helpful suggestions for improvement. Thank you to Bishops Ken Carter, Mark Webb, Minerva Carcaño, and Mike Lowry, as well as Professor Bob Tuttle and Rev. Varlyna Wright. Bishop Sudarshana Devadhar gave very helpful suggestions with regard to the way we speak of persons of other faith traditions so as not to perpetuate imperialistic language. I greatly appreciate his input.

I am especially grateful to my wife, Tammie. Her support and encouragement during the months it took to complete this project were filled with grace, love, and patience.

I dedicate this book to Hugo Urcola and to all my friends and colleagues of the Evangelical Methodist Church of Argentina. Reverend Urcola served as my supervising pastor during the entire time I lived in Argentina. He has been a lifelong friend and colleague and a tireless communicator of the gospel of Jesus Christ.

His support and guidance during my early years have helped shape all the years of my service in the church. There are no words to express how profoundly grateful I am for his friendship, mentoring, and support. *Gracias, Hugo. ¡Sos inolvidable!*

INTRODUCTION

To reach our communities with the gospel of Jesus Christ, we need, more than ever before in the Western world, a missionary mindset. Our context for ministry is less and less familiar with Christianity, so it feels more and more like a foreign mission field. One of the first things we need to do is overcome any reticence with the term *missionary*. I should know; I bore the label myself.

Two years after graduating from seminary, I was headed to Argentina to serve as a "missionary." I disdained the term at the time. I had heard too many stories of how missionaries had messed things up for indigenous people. I preferred the term *fraternal worker*, the English translation of the term *obrero fraternal* employed by the church that received me, the Evangelical Methodist Church of Argentina. My wife, our three-month-old son, and I boarded a flight from Miami to Buenos Aires in the fall of 1978. After serving briefly as an interim pastor for an English-speaking church while learning the Spanish language, we spent the majority of our first three years in a small rural city, Dolores, 120 miles south of the city of Buenos Aires.

Only nine years before, the Argentine Methodists had graduated from being a "mission church" of The United Methodist Church to being a church on its own. While still connected historically and practically to its mother church in the United States, it now governed itself and elected its own leaders. They had requested a pastor from the United States and preferred the term *fraternal worker* because it honored their choice and autonomy. I readily saw myself in this role—a worker sent by one sister church to help another sister church, and so I, too, embraced the term.

My home church back in New Jersey referred to me as a "missionary," though. They would not have understood any other term, so in my correspondence with folks back home, I used the default *missionary*.

Identifying Our Default Culture

The classic dilemma for a missionary is to learn where one's own cultural trappings interfere with the presentation of the gospel in a culture different from one's own. A person with a missionary mindset is aware of his or her own culture while learning as much as possible about the new culture served.

The term *default culture* is borrowed from the world of computers. Default settings are the original settings on the computer when it comes out of the box. As we add programs, these settings often change. We might adjust them to better fit our needs and habits. Sometimes defaults are changed inadvertently and end up causing problems. For example, we might upload incompatible software systems that compromise the operation. Sometimes the entire operation becomes so compromised that the only apparent solution is to hit the reset button and return the computer to its original, or default, settings.

Like computer software, we have defaults—assumptions and habits about every arena of life that we have adopted from our families, work environment, church, and the wider culture. Our tendency to carry our default culture into a new community can produce harmless and sometimes humorous results, but it has too often misfired. The church I served in New Jersey in the late eighties resisted my predecessor's insistence on purchasing a computer and copier. They preferred the default system of a type-writer and a mimeograph. We are talking about *change* here: our resistance to it and our tendency to cling to what we have always known. Sometimes the only defense is the clichéd response, "We have always done it that way."

Gaining clarity about our own "default culture" when serving in a new context is an invitation to consider what needs to be changed. While living in Dolores, I began to run for exercise through its streets. My "default" garb for running included shorts, a T-shirt, and a pair of running shoes. Dolores, evidently, was unprepared for my running garb. I received reports from members of comments from townspeople about the scantily clad new pastor of the Methodist church. Soon I was wearing sweatpants!

A classic example of navigating the change inherent in one's default culture occurred in China in the nineteenth century, when missionaries from England attempted to convert the Chinese to Christianity. The English missionaries continued to dress as they did in England, and they lived apart from the Chinese, in a "missionary compound." The Chinese looked upon these well-intentioned people as strange, and the missionaries themselves began to wonder if they would ever gain acceptance.

Hudson Taylor arrived in China as a young missionary and before long began to take an entirely different approach. He moved out of the compound and into a dwelling among the Chinese people. He discarded his English clothing in favor of indigenous garb, learned to speak the language well, and even cut his hair except for a small ponytail. He managed to gain a hearing among Chinese people and was able to sow the seeds of the gospel.

I have had my own experiences with defaults that cause problems. I grew up in metropolitan New York and from early childhood attended a United Methodist church in an affluent, middle-class suburb of the big city. My default understanding of Christ and the church is thoroughly imbued with the culture of this area.

When I began my term in Dolores, I left those familiar surroundings. My task was to turn around a church that had been in decline for many years. The church, even by Argentine standards, was made up of poor people. Many lived in homes without running water.

In the daily work navigating the waters of cross-cultural understanding, I learned that "you can take me out of my country but you can't take my country out of me." In other words, I was serving in a new and different setting, but inevitably my own cultural default settings were bound to surface. One of the first mistakes I made was to print bulletins for worship. Argentina was a literate country where even the poor had access to free public education. I learned later, though, that many of the older members of the congregation I served could not read but they were embarrassed to say anything to me. Because I was using bulletins, they could not participate fully in worship. When I realized what I had done, I felt bad. I did not want to embarrass or do anything to make these older members feel shamed. But I had always been used to printed bulletins. I had relied on a default setting for church without entering deeply enough into my congregation's world to understand the people and their culture. When I realized what had happened, I quietly did away with the bulletins.

A LONG-STANDING CHALLENGE

Presenting Christ in a new culture has been a challenge for the church since biblical times. We only need review the debate among the apostles during the first council of the Church in Jerusalem to understand this key moment in the life of the early church. Luke reported on the council in Acts 15:1-21, and Paul discussed it in his letter to the Galatians.

Acts reports, without going into the dirty details, on a council held in Jerusalem dealing with the controversy about whether non-Jewish followers of Jesus had to follow Jewish law and cultural practices. Remember there was not yet a separation between Judaism and Christianity. The early Christians believed that the reform introduced by Jesus broadened the reach of Judaism to people of all nations. The separation into two religions came later.

Paul addressed these issues in his first letter to the Corinthians, as well as with the Galatians.[1] In Galatians 2:11-14, Paul reported that he had taken Peter to task for the way he had behaved among Jews and Gentiles in Antioch. Peter had previously eaten with Gentiles, but at Antioch, Peter had withdrawn from their company, fearful that "the Judaizers" would disapprove of his fraternization. Paul confronted Peter for his hypocrisy. Both Paul and Peter believed that Jesus opened access to God for all people, Jews and non-Jews. But Peter had sat with the circumcised, giving the impression that the uncircumcised were somehow not equal to Jews.

While Peter assented intellectually to the notion of equality between Jewish and Gentile followers of Jesus, when the two groups came together for food and table fellowship, Peter defaulted to Jewish law and his own culture. This was a tricky situation indeed, because it was nearly impossible to separate Jewish law from Jewish culture. The one gives rise to the other. They are inextricably linked. The argument, then, of that first council, had everything to do with distinguishing between law and culture.

Paul emphatically believed that in Christ the distinctions that separate us from one another fall away (see Galatians 3:28). If we oblige followers to first become Jewish (people of the circumcision as law and culture), posited Paul, then we lose the power and significance of the freedom that Jesus introduced into the world of religion. Jesus invited people into an unencumbered relationship with God. Paul's answer to the question, Do Gentiles need to become Jews before following Christ? was a resounding no.

This was a defining moment for the mission of Jesus' followers. Would they accept the broader platform advocated by Paul, which allowed for direct access to a relationship with Jesus? Or would Jews, like Peter, default to Jewish practice and expect non-Jews to comply with Jewish law and culture? The Christian missionary endeavor hinged on these questions. The Council of Jerusalem discerned that Jesus' Jewish followers were being called to give up their default. The council sent a delegation to Antioch with a letter, reporting to the young church, "It has seemed good to the Holy Spirit and to us to impose on you no further burdens than these essentials" (Acts 15:28). We can gain insight into Paul's and the council's position by turning to the Great Commission.

LESSONS FROM THE EARLY CHURCH

In the Great Commission (Matt. 28:19-20), the Greek word translated "nations" is *ethné*, the root word for "ethnicity." Jesus commands followers to go to all ethnicities. In most cases, *ethné* is used to refer to people who are non-Jews. Going to all nations, in this sense, means proclaiming the God of Israel, the God of Abraham and Sarah and Moses and Miriam, to the people beyond Israel. What Jesus has done through his teachings, life, death, and resurrection is open wide the doors, inviting non-Jewish nations to embrace the Jewish God.

Matthew, who wrote to a Jewish Christian community, is proclaiming to his people that they need to take Jesus beyond their own tribe. The commission is to go beyond our own boundaries and proclaim the good news that all people are invited to believe in and embrace the God of Abraham and Jesus. This commission does not abrogate the religion of the people of Israel. It is a call to extend the reach of that religion to ethnicities around the world.

Ethnicity houses culture. It references a person's race. Culture embodies the traditions, practices, and accepted behaviors of that ethnicity transmitted from generation to generation. In the twenty-first century and the context of an ever-growing world migration that is increasing diversity in the Americas and Europe, making disciples of all *ethné* takes on an even broader meaning. We are invited to develop a missionary mindset: to embrace and love people whose cultural context is different from our own. From the beginning, as the controversy dealt with by the Jerusalem Council demonstrates, the challenge for followers of Jesus has been to navigate from our tribe and culture to present the gospel to a tribe and culture different from our own.

The history of Christianity is filled with good and bad examples of ways to live this out. In the Americas, Christianity followed on the heels of death and destruction of native peoples by European conquerors. The cross was introduced along with the sword. The Spaniards and Portuguese conquered a territory, sometimes settling into the land, but then systematically "evangelized" the people who lived there. The conquerors deemed the natives barbarous and pagan races.[2] The triumphalist missionaries who accompanied conquerors tore down indigenous belief systems. The Christian workers believed they were doing the right thing by presenting the gospel to them but were complicit in the harshness and cruelty of European conquerors, which led to the death of whole populations.

Christians perpetrated atrocities against people of other faiths not only in the Americas, but throughout the world. The expansion of Christianity included the holy war against Muslims in medieval times and the Inquisition in Spain. In Africa, Christian missions, by retaining their default understanding of English law, wreaked havoc on the system for preserving order among indigenous peoples. As church historian Diana Butler Bass has pointed out, a review of this history would make even church-going Christians "agree with the atheist Christopher Hitchens when he claims, 'Religion poisons everything.'"[3]

The logical question in light of a history replete with pejorative examples of Christian mission is, did anything *good* come out of missionary engagement? Are there any examples at all that speak to the way of Jesus rather than to the way of culture-negating priests and ministers who went out in his name? Many Christian leaders working in the area of congregational development—both starting new communities of faith and revitalizing existing ones—believe there *are* good, better, and best missionary practices. It is to these examples we will turn as we build a framework for a modern-day missionary mindset.

Adopting a Missionary Mindset

I learned some things as a missionary that I think are relevant to challenges faced by churches in the twenty-first century. The things I had to learn—another language, an alternative culture, unfamiliar music, new art, a different way of dressing, a change in my mode of transportation, exotic food and beverages—were all bits and pieces of a new way of approaching life and connecting with people. I was well aware that I was a foreigner in a new country. The better I learned how to speak their language and the sooner I learned to love their food and beverages and the more I blended in by wearing clothes like theirs, the better chance I had of getting a hearing from the people I came in contact with. I needed to learn a "missionary mindset."

Our current context for ministry in the United States feels foreign enough to many church leaders that our role seems a lot like that of a missionary. We are surrounded by a culture estranged from the Christian context that was present thirty or forty years ago. Researchers George Barna and David Kinnaman refer to the current U.S. culture as "churchless."[4] As many as 70 percent of younger people do not find the church either relevant or meaningful and therefore see no reason to attend. Those of us who have grown up in the church are called upon to learn the language of the people with whom we live and value their music and art and way of dressing and the many other bits and pieces that help us get closer to a people we want to communicate with, learn about, and love.

We are called to love our neighbors in all of their diversity and understand the similarities and differences between our way of living and theirs. After all, as the most quoted verse of the Bible says, "God so loved the world that he gave his only Son" (John 3:16). God came in the person of Jesus not because God loved the *church* but because God loved the *world* and sought to show the world the way, the truth, and the life. Since we church leaders live with so many *churchless* people, we are to take this love of God to heart and love the world as God loves it.

Now, many years after my eight-year sojourn in a foreign country as a missionary, I am remembering the things I had to do to be accepted there and how important it is to figure out how to identify with the daily life of the people with whom I live. Learning to identify with the people in our midst is important to church leaders who want to support new communities of faith so they can better relate to their contexts. While identifying with a new culture may come more easily to new church planters, because of their natural tendency to focus outward on those who are not yet part of a community of faith, existing churches also need to learn a missionary mindset. They must find new ways to relate to the people living in their communities. But all of us can learn from those who have served as missionaries through the years. When we draw upon the practices of these servants, we can gain insight into the principles that help us relate to people across cultures and languages, even when they are living in our own communities.

The challenge for Christians in today's world is to earn enough trust from the people we intend to serve that the gospel message can be heard and heeded. We approach our mission field as if we were from some different country and learning a new way of communicating, a new culture, a new way to connect people to the gospel of Jesus Christ. *This* is a missionary mindset.

THE CALL OF THE GOSPEL

Despite my shortsightedness about printing bulletins for a church with illiterate members, the congregation in Dolores extended much grace, understanding, and patience toward me, for which I am forever grateful. Still, I had to make some effort to enter their culture. One thing I did that helped bridge the divide between my default culture and my congregation's was to learn to enjoy the Argentine drink called *maté*. It is a hot, tealike beverage drunk from a gourd (also called a *maté*) with a metal straw (a *bombilla*). Offering maté was an indigenous form of hospitality. It would have been rude for people not to offer me a maté. I had been encouraged in missionary orientation to accept such forms of hospitality and so readily accepted.

When I visited parishioners in their homes, I was offered a gourd filled with loose tea (called *yerba*) and hot water. One drinks it down and returns it to the host or hostess, who refills it and passes it on to the next person. The ritual is repeated as the maté makes the rounds among the people present, much like a Native American peace pipe. All of us drank from the same gourd using the same metal straw.

My default culture had taught me to worry about germs as the maté was passed from person to person. In an attempt to embrace a culture not my own, I suspended these concerns in order to enter my parishioners' culture. I learned to love to drink maté and the sense of community and hospitality it engendered. By accepting this hospitality, I was able to gain acceptance, despite speaking the language with an accent and trying to impose printed bulletins in worship.

We all have a default culture that is firmly embedded in who we are. With a missionary mindset, we recognize our own default culture and work to go beyond it to embrace the culture of those with whom we are sharing the gospel of Jesus Christ. I believe that the apostle Paul addressed this issue when he wrote to the Corinthians:

> For though I am free with respect to all, I have made myself a slave to all, so that I might win more of them. To the Jews I became as a Jew, in order to win Jews. To those under the law I became as one under the law (though I myself am not under the law) so that I might win those under the law. To those outside the law I became as one outside the law (though I am not free from God's law but am under Christ's law) so that I might win those outside the law. To the weak I became weak, so that I might win the weak. I have become all things to all people, that I might by all means save some. (1 Cor. 9:19-22)

It would be a mistake to read into this passage that Paul somehow compromised his own beliefs to win people for Christ. Paul was not saying that he would violate Jewish tradition when relating to non-Jews. Rather, Paul sought a beginning point for the relationship with someone outside his default culture, a way to relate to the "other" on common ground so conversation could ensue. He opened a portal so Christ could enter into the relationship and begin the work of transformation.

With a missionary mindset, we gain an appreciation for the importance of relationships. We can learn from the apostle Paul that when we find the right starting place in a relationship, the Christ in us can begin to recognize the Christ in the other. It is in the relationship and the conversation that Christ has a chance to enter both evangelizer and evangelized with his transforming Spirit.

Essentials of the Gospel Message

Most important, a missionary mindset is clear about the essentials of the gospel we proclaim. We affirm these essentials in the simple, easily remembered statement often repeated when communities of faith gather for holy Communion: *Christ has died. Christ is risen. Christ shall come again.*

Christ has died. We give witness to the fact that Christ died. He sacrificed his life for us. He died for our individual sins and the sins of humanity, so that we might live a new life in him and so that all creation might be reconciled to God. Especially when these words are spoken in the context of Communion, we remember our own sinfulness and our complicity in the sinfulness of humanity that made it necessary for Christ to die for our sins. He died not only for the individual sins we have committed but for the sins of humanity, including the systemic evil of tribes and nations and of principalities and powers. We are moved to confess our sins and ask God for forgiveness. We can affirm, along with the apostle Paul, that he died so that "we too might walk in newness of life" (Rom. 6:4). The death of Jesus was the completion of a life fully lived so that we can see in Jesus the way to live our own lives.

28

Christ is risen. A missionary mindset leads us to proclaim that through the divine initiative of God, Creator of the universe, God sent God's own Son in the person of Jesus to save humanity from eternal death. Christ defeated death through the resurrection. This gives us hope that through our relationship with Christ we can overcome the evil of the world. We *so* trust God in Christ that we live with confidant joy that God will defeat the forces of evil in the world. The gospel of Luke tells the story of how Jesus broke bread with two of his followers after they had walked on the road to Emmaus. At the breaking of the bread, these followers exclaimed that "their eyes were opened, and they recognized him" (Luke 24:31). When we affirm that Christ is risen, we celebrate the wonder that he defeated death. We move from guilt over our sin and grief over the many manifestations of evil in the world to celebration of the resurrection. We celebrate that we can see Christ in each other as members together of a community of faith.

Christ shall come again. A missionary mindset embraces the affirmation that God's will and God's way will ultimately prevail over humankind's inept attempts to create world order. We also affirm that in the spirit of the Christ who lives in us, we become partners with God in bringing God's future kingdom to reality. This is a challenging call, especially in a world torn by violence, evil, and hatred. Our trust in God's ultimate victory in Christ gives us hope for the future and encouragement to work with God and others to bring about a world that is transformed by God's love.

A missionary mindset seeks to invite others to embrace this same faith that Christ died for our sins, that he rose so we may live a new life, and that God will ultimately claim victory over the forces of evil in the world. We proclaim the good news of the kingdom that Jesus inaugurated with his presence on earth and invite others to give their allegiance to Jesus and his kingdom.

As we delve into the details of a missionary mindset, we are invited to remember the essentials of the gospel and to be clear about what we proclaim—the good news of Jesus Christ.

YOUR TURN:
QUESTIONS FOR REFLECTION AND DISCUSSION

1. How would you describe your default culture?

2. How does an understanding of your default culture help answer the question, "Who am I?"?

3. How would a "missionary mindset" help you relate to people who live in your community?

4. How do the issues addressed by the first Jerusalem Council help us understand the challenge of relating to people of a different culture?

5. What is your understanding of the essentials of the gospel, and why is it important to have clarity about them?

1

REMEMBERING
E. STANLEY JONES

*Jesus didn't die to make a difference in the world; he died
to make a different world. And I think that God has raised
up E. Stanley Jones for this time, even more than the time
that he lived, to show us how to make a different world.*[1]

—LEN SWEET

He was a friend of Mahatma Gandhi, and his writings deeply
influenced Martin Luther King Jr. He was twice nominated for the Nobel Peace Prize. He was a confidant of President
Franklin Delano Roosevelt and an inspiration to Billy Graham. He
was described as the greatest missionary since the apostle Paul.
He wrote twenty-nine books that were translated into thirty languages. His first of ten devotional books, *Victorious Living*, sold
more than 1 million copies after it came out in 1936. In 1938 *Time*
magazine called him "the world's greatest missionary evangelist."

His name was E. Stanley Jones.

I had heard of E. Stanley Jones but had never read any of his books until I came across *The Christ of the American Road* in the library of First Methodist Church in Rosario, Argentina. Jones had been in the United States on a visit in 1941. From that volume, I learned that among his many religious activities, he "was trying in a humble way over many months [to serve] as a go-between to avert the war between Japan and America—'an adventure in failure.'"[2] He would be nominated for the Nobel Peace Prize for his efforts to bring peace among nations in 1962 and 1963.[3] On December 4, 1941, he had a face-to-face conversation with President Franklin Delano Roosevelt, in which Jones pleaded with him to send a letter to Emperor Hirohito to find a peaceful resolution to conflict between the United States and Japan. Roosevelt wrote the letter, which arrived in Japan hours too late on December 7.

When the attack on Pearl Harbor occurred, Jones learned that he would not be able to return to India as he had hoped. A travel ban had been instituted, and he was also denied a visa by England due to his forthright support of India's independence. Thus, he spent extended time in the United States, where he was able to establish Christian ashrams. *The Christ of the American Road* was also a fruit of that time. Jones addressed the American context in much the same way as his earlier book, *The Christ of the Indian Road*, addressed the Indian context.

Published in 1944, *The Christ of the American Road* laid out what the United States needed to do to live out the promise of the reign of God. Among other subjects, it addressed head-on the sin of racism in the United States. Drawing on his friendship with and knowledge of Mahatma Gandhi, Jones outlined a way that Christians—both black and white—could put an end to the insidious racism in the country.

- He advocated for educating the populace that the words of the Declaration of Independence—"liberty and justice for all"—mean for *all*.
- He called for a nationwide curriculum in public schools on race appreciation.
- He called on Christian churches to welcome persons of other races into membership.
- He called for a nationwide campaign to do away with discriminatory laws.

If all of these actions failed to bring an end to racism, Jones wrote:

> Then [African Americans], probably joined by whites, may have to resort to nonviolent non-cooperation by picking out certain injustices and then, through volunteers trained in nonviolent methods, refusing to obey these specific injustices and taking the consequences of that civil disobedience. This would be an appeal to the conscience of the country.[4]

I was stunned when I first read those words. *He wrote this in 1944!* He foretold the coming civil rights movement in America and the nonviolent methodology that Martin Luther King Jr. embraced.

I sought out other books that E. Stanley Jones wrote and was fortunate that the church's small library, located in a *salón* next to the sanctuary, included many of Jones's other writings, as well as theological classics of the twentieth century. For years, First Church had served the English-speaking community of Rosario, which included the descendants of British railroad operators and English-speaking expatriates. Only ten years before my arrival, they had discontinued the English worship service and had begun worshipping only in Spanish.

Among the library's holdings was *Christ's Alternative to Communism*, which Jones had written in 1935 and Carlos Gattinoni, bishop of the Evangelical Methodist Church of Argentina from 1969 to 1977, had translated into Spanish. Jones objected to communism because of its lack of liberty and its materialistic atheism. But he also respected communism's attempt to found a society on cooperation. Jones was harshly criticized because he took communism seriously and described it in objective terms. I soon learned that Stanley Jones also took great care to learn about the other religions of the world. To present Christ as an alternative to Buddhism or the religion of Islam or Hinduism, just as in his study of communism, he first valued the religion enough to understand its contributions and accurately present its tenets.

Gattinoni was also the uncle of Anely Urcola, my superintendent's wife. I had met Carlos on several occasions and even spent my first Christmas Eve in Argentina with his extended family. Tall, lean, with snow-white hair, the now-retired bishop was perfectly fluent in English, though he always spoke to me in Spanish, knowing full well that I needed the practice. He was sharp in dress and speech, quick-witted, and ever ready to share a self-deprecating story that was at once humorous and instructive.

"Oh yes," he told me when we met up in Buenos Aires several months after I discovered the books, "Stanley Jones was well-known and well respected in this part of the world. His books were very popular."

"Did you know him personally?" I asked.

"Of course," said Gattinoni. "He came to Argentina several times." And then Bishop Gattinoni told me about a visit Jones had unexpectedly made one hot summer in the 1950s.

"He had been scheduled to lead a weeklong spiritual retreat in Uruguay. When his plane arrived in Montevideo, he found out that there had been a miscommunication along the way and the Uruguayans were not prepared for him. He had come a long way and, of course, back then, it took months to exchange letters. It was a Saturday in January, and he called me from Uruguay to see if we might be able to arrange something in Buenos Aires on the spur of the moment."

I listened to the bishop's story enraptured.

"I told him we would do what we could, and yes, we could arrange for him to preach in the evening at First Church in the city center. I said that many people were on vacation and that it was hot and we would not have time to advertise, but we would try."

Jones boarded a ferry to cross the seventy-mile-wide *Rio de la Plata*, which separates Uruguay from Argentina. He arrived on Sunday morning.

"I called several of our pastors and friends from other denominations," said Gattinoni. "We announced in church on Sunday morning that E. Stanley Jones would be preaching at First Church beginning that evening. I urged them to spread the news and to pray for the event and to invite friends and to come. Quite frankly, I was worried that we would get a very poor turnout."

Bishop Gattinoni smiled at me and with a twinkle said, "It must have been the prayers. The church was packed that night—standing room only. The word-of-mouth news spread quickly. It remained packed every night for a week. There was something about his preaching style—even with my translation—that had people coming forward to enter into a relationship with Jesus Christ."

Gattinoni's testimony of the personal magnetism of Stanley Jones inspired me. I began to read every book of Jones that I could get my hands on. I devoured *The Christ of the Indian Road*, published in 1925.[5] Jones had served as a missionary in India starting in 1907, and the book recounted experiences and awakenings that occurred after he had been in India for a decade. "He could be writing this *today*," I remember commenting. His insights, even ninety years later, give helpful direction for Christian leaders who want to reach people in a context of people of other faith expressions.

Many of Jones's fellow missionaries served the lower castes and outcastes, the most vulnerable in Indian society. They lived a life of poverty, always at the margins. The religion of Jesus Christ was particularly good news for these people, offering hope in their downtrodden existence. Hindu theology, or at least the popular understanding of it, taught that one's lot in life was the result of how a person lived a previous incarnation. Life was a succession of incarnations. Thus, if people were poor and outcast, they deserved their fate based on the way they had lived a previous lifetime. Christianity offered hope and a belief that because they were children of God, they were of infinite worth.

Jones felt called to relate to higher-caste people. A Hindu government official had asked Jones quite pointedly, "Why have you gone only to the lower castes? Why haven't you come to us?" Jones replied that he and others had supposed the higher-caste members did not want them. The Hindu replied, "It is a mistake. We want you if you will come in the *right way*."[6] Jones remarked that ever since hearing this comment, he had eagerly sought "the right way."

What would be the "right way"?

Jones concluded that if he were to relate to a people in a context of other faith expressions, even those who questioned the validity of Christianity, he had "to be a Christian with all the fearless implications of that term."[7] If we want to share the faith that means so much to us, we would be wise to deepen our understanding of discipleship and strive to close the gap between who we ought to be and who we really are. It is a humbling task. To reach the goal of such wholeness and congruity requires a lifelong journey fraught with missteps and egregious errors. Even the thought of trying to achieve what John Wesley called "Christian perfection" should drive us to our knees in prayer.

When Jones realized the enormity of this calling, he at first recoiled. "I was painfully conscious that I was not intellectually prepared for it. I was the more painfully conscious that I was not Christian enough to do what the situation demanded. And most depressing of all, I was physically broken."[8] Jones had worked nearly nonstop for eight years doing a variety of ministry work, including pastoring an English-speaking church, leading a publishing house, regularly visiting poor villages, and serving as a superintendent of a large area.[9]

He experienced several physical collapses both in India and while preaching a Sunday morning service on board a ship to the United States. Jones was burned out. Not even a year's furlough back in the United States restored him. On his way back to India, he stopped in the Philippines to meet with students, and once again he collapsed. He was eager to return to India, yet still felt totally drained. Upon arrival in India he sought further restoration at a mountain retreat. But healing was elusive. "My health was shattered," he wrote. "Here I was facing a call and task and yet utterly unprepared for it in every possible way."[10] He felt totally overwhelmed by the enormity of the ministry to which he was called and wondered if he should return to the States and go back to work on a farm.

At that time, which he described as his darkest hour, he went to his knees. During a meeting he attended in Lucknow, India, Jones confessed to God that he was "done for." He had reached the end of his resources. It was during this prayer that Jones heard a message from God that spoke to his innermost being. He called this message *the Voice*. He heard the Voice say to him, *If you will turn that over to me and not worry about it, I will take care of it.* Jones responded, "Lord, I close the bargain right here." He sensed a peace come into his heart and a huge weight lifted.[11]

After years of physical, emotional, and spiritual exhaustion, Jones kept praying until the Spirit touched him and restored him. He referred to his experience as the Touch and was so touched that he was able to move forward in ministry and never again experienced such a long stretch of exhaustion. He was energized and now fully ready for the challenge of communicating the gospel to India's higher castes. He committed himself thoroughly to this calling and, finally, felt ready for the challenge.

What, then, did Jones discover about the "right way" to approach people who did not identify with Christianity? And what can we learn from him for our own day's challenges?

At first Jones reflected on several methodologies that were practiced in his day—and are still used today—but which he would eventually reject. He did not want to tear down the belief systems of others in order to build up and replace them with Christian beliefs. Such a method is arrogant and disrespectful. He refused to persuade others that Christianity somehow "fulfills the ancient faiths," as if it somehow summed up the religions of the world. He also would have disagreed with the popular tendency today to dismiss the differences in belief systems by asserting, "All religions lead to the same thing." Nor did he want to attempt a subtler manipulation that starts off addressing a general subject of common interest only to morph into a Christian message and appeal. This is perhaps the sliest form of proselytism that disguises hidden agendas with an air of openness.

Jones sought a better way, one that built on principles without attacking anyone's belief system. He wanted to connect with others honestly and openly with no hidden agendas, subtle manipulations, or sideways approaches through "safe subjects." He wanted to bring people to a roundtable where everyone could speak to his or her truth without anyone assuming a position of superiority.[12] He encouraged open, honest dialogue where questions could be asked and difficult issues faced. He believed that "Christianity must be defined as Christ, not . . . Western Civilization, not even the system built around him in the West, but Christ himself."[13]

Jones sought a Christ in an *Indian* setting. He advocated "the Christ of the Indian Road," not the Christ of his country or culture or of his native prejudices and practices. He knew instinctually that he needed to go beyond his default culture, the Christianity he'd learned growing up in a Methodist church in Baltimore, Maryland. He knew that doing so takes commitment as well as self-awareness. Jones knew that we must be willing to let loose the cultural ties that we carry within us. While we cannot extricate ourselves from our own culture, we can be sufficiently aware of our baggage that we are willing to make the effort to embrace another's culture, one different from our own default.

Jones took to heart and kept in mind what the Indian literary genius Rabindranath Tagore said: "When missionaries bring their truth to a strange land, unless they bring it in the form of homage it is not accepted and should not be. The manner of offering it to you must not be at all discordant with your own national thought and your self-respect."[14] Tagore sought honesty, authenticity, and transparency from Christian missionaries.

The key for Jones was presenting what he called "an untrammeled Christ."[15] He put himself in the challenging position of speaking to the truth he knew in Christ in dialogue with learned Hindus, Muslims, Buddhists, and skeptics, who in turn spoke to the truth they knew in their religions. All of this was done in an atmosphere of civility, mutual respect, and humility. Jones kept in mind the greater good of humanity who would benefit from this kind of conversation.

Jones believed that this approach was grounded in scripture. He quoted Paul's Second Letter to the Corinthians: "We refuse to practice cunning or to falsify God's word; but by the open statement of the truth we commend ourselves to the conscience of everyone in the sight of God" (2 Cor. 4:2). Jones believed that "Jesus appeals to the soul as light appeals to the eye, as truth fits the conscience, as beauty speaks to the aesthetic nature."[16]

Jones believed that Christ needed to be discovered in India by Indians as one walking an Indian road. When we transfer this principle to our own day, then we are invited to desire a similar outcome—that the people of our city or town discover the Christ who walks with them, who is recognizable among them, and who fully understands their context.

LOVE AND "THE RIGHT WAY"

Jones's struggle to find the "right way" to present Christ in his missionary context must be our struggle as well today, for we also live in a missionary context where many have not heard the gospel in terms they can understand. Just as Jones wrestled with the question of *the right way*, contemporary missionaries need to discern what the right approach would be in our context. In the twenty-first-century United States, the context includes descendants of Hindus and Muslims whom Jones related to a century ago as well as what recent demographers term "nones," that growing part of the population who do not identify with any religion at all.[17]

Our challenge is to present what Jones called "the untrammeled Christ." Jesus continues to capture the imagination of people. People speak against the actions of the church, past and present. Yet, they continue to be fascinated with and attracted to Jesus, the friend of the marginalized, the poor, the outcast, children, and women. If our focus is on Jesus, we are more likely to gain a hearing. Our challenge is to focus our witness on the person and ministry of Jesus.

We are invited, then, to plumb the depths of what it means to present an "untrammeled Christ" today. There is no better way than to take to heart the Great Commandment of Jesus to "love the Lord your God with all your heart, and with all your soul, and with all your mind'" . . . and to "love your neighbor as yourself" (Matt. 22:37-39). Our approach must be permeated with the love of Christ in our hearts. As Paul wrote, "Clothe yourselves with love" (Col. 3:14). With this love, we care deeply for all people, whether they profess faith or not, whether an ardent follower of a religion or avowed atheist or agnostic. Our involvement with people begins by loving them and thus valuing them as human beings. It is through this love that we respect, dignify, and honor their humanity and desire the very best for their souls. *This* is the "right way" to approach people today.

As we seek to transmit the good news of Jesus in today's world, we would be wise to learn from the example of E. Stanley Jones. We are invited to adopt a *missionary mindset* that affords us the chance to communicate the gospel in ways that will gain a hearing among those who are estranged from a community of faith, as well as those who have never had any interest: the unchurched, dechurched, and nones.

How can we create a safe space where honest exchange can occur in an atmosphere of respect and love? E. Stanley Jones brought people of different faiths and belief systems to the roundtable of conversation, which elicited true openness to one another. "I have noted the change that comes over the group in the first ten minutes," wrote Jones. "Many have come fortified and ready to enter a battle of wits and to uphold their religious system against all comers. But immediately the atmosphere changes, a deep seriousness comes over them, for here the battle drops to levels deeper than a mere battle of words or of ideas—drops down to where we meet life—we are at grips with life."[18]

Jones believed that at stake in such dialogues was life itself. Does our religion—whichever it may be—bring well-being? Does it help human beings live good lives? Does it bring happiness? "Religion is to speak to life," he wrote. Do we have answers to life's questions? Or are we merely living out traditions of our belief systems that now are out of sync with reality? Can we go deeper with one another to unveil the meaning of life? Can we let, as Jones so eloquently stated, "deep . . . speak to deep"?[19]

Jones trusted the power and truth of the gospel of Christ and became vulnerable to others, laying the truth he knew beside their truth. In this way, Jones manifested a missionary mindset that valued the people he encountered—loved them—and in this way gave honor to the One who died for us so that we might live; who arose for us that we might have new life; who will come again in final victory to defeat the forces of evil in the world.

From my reading of E. Stanley Jones and following his methodology, I have distilled what I believe are transferable principles that can inform a missionary mindset as today's Christian leaders and church planters reach out to their communities with the untrammeled Jesus.

Each of the following chapters will focus on one of these "right ways" to reach our communities.

- Prayer: keeping our focus on God
- Self-awareness: understanding who we are
- Listening: taking the risk to understand
- Humility: looking to the interests of others
- Love: valuing humanity
- Planting like Paul: learning from Roland Allen

- Kingdom: living and breathing the gospel
- Trust: believing in the power of the gospel

These principles will inform the ensuing chapters as we seek to delineate the missionary mindset we need to adopt as we plant a new church or revitalize an existing one. As we dig deeper into each of the themes gleaned from the work of E. Stanley Jones, we will also draw on experiences from the mission—both my own and others'.

I remember vividly how Bishop Carlos Gattinoni recounted with enthusiasm and joy Stanley Jones's visit to Buenos Aires and the way Jones mesmerized crowds of people who came to hear him speak. There was something about his authenticity that drew people not to Jones himself but to the Christ who walks our road with us, who speaks to the depth of our yearnings, and who helps us live life to its fullest. Jones asked simple questions of people: how is your faith (or lack thereof) helping you to live life? Is it working? Are you experiencing the life abundant promised by the gospel? Those same questions ring true today.

YOUR TURN:
QUESTIONS FOR REFLECTION AND DISCUSSION

1. Compare the methodologies that E. Stanley Jones rejected with current approaches to evangelism.

2. What religions are represented in your community? What do you know about them?

3. What percentage of the population in your area considers themselves *nones*?

4. How will you and your study group be in prayer for one another as you work through this book?

2

PRAYER
KEEPING OUR FOCUS ON GOD

*Gracious Christ, teach me to pray. If I fall down in this area,
I fall down everywhere—anemia spreads through my whole
being. Give me the mind to pray, the love to pray, the will to
pray. Let prayer be the aroma of every act, the atmosphere
of every thought, my native air. In your name. Amen.*

—E. STANLEY JONES[1]

In the center of one of the largest cities in Argentina, I discovered an oasis. We lived in Rosario, Argentina's third-largest city, with a metro population over a million. Though I served a school eight blocks away and a church farther away still, I lived at the downtown church campus of the Methodist church. There were two parsonages, one at the back of the property and one in front. A splendid outdoor courtyard separated the parsonages, and adjacent stood a sanctuary that easily accommodated three hundred worshippers.

On mornings before heading off to the school where I served as chaplain, I walked out the front door of my parsonage, descended a stairway to the outdoor courtyard, and then walked toward the street and to the side entrance of the sanctuary. Once inside, I headed to the front pew. I heard birds chirping from the windows that faced the courtyard and the screeching of city bus brakes behind me. I sat and listened for several minutes before reading scripture and journaling. The ceiling of the sanctuary rose high, and though it was simple in design, with clear windows, wooden pews, and an unadorned chancel, I sensed that I sat in sacred space.

Many mornings I failed to enter the sanctuary. A *prie-dieu*, a single-person kneeler with a tilted shelf, served as my desk as I kneeled at the front of the chancel and listened and read and wrote. After meditating in silence for several minutes, I waited until the sounds of birds overcame the sounds of the city. I breathed in the fragrance of wood, and on sunny days I looked for the stream of sunlight coming from the windows high up the wall.

My attempt at following a daily practice of scripture reading and prayer hit and missed. I struggled with forming a habit that carried me forward day after day. Sometimes I stayed in bed too long, preferring more sleep. Other times, the demands of young children, still in diapers, took precedence over time apart. Yet, when I made the time and followed the exercise, I felt at peace. I knew it was important, for it helped me live in a more balanced, whole way. I always received a blessing from scripture verses and gained spiritual insight from special readings. It afforded me an opportunity to pray for the people in my local church and for the present day's state of affairs. It centered me for the day ahead. It reminded me of my calling as a follower of Jesus. Thus, in spite of my inconsistency, I kept returning to the well of prayer.

I did not serve this church. My front-parsonage neighbor, Hugo Urcola, who was also my supervising minister, pastored this church. Occasionally he peeked into the worship center from his adjacent office, trying not to be noticed. He respected this time of personal devotion and wished not to interfere. He knew that this was my oasis, my "quiet space." For me, it was filled with majesty and holiness and splendor. Because I did not spend my Sundays in this sanctuary, it was the more resplendent and mysterious.

I used a resource I had received in the mail from the Upper Room in Nashville, *A Guide to Prayer for Ministers and Other Servants*, edited by Rueben Job and Norman Shawchuck.[2] Each day I would follow the book's outline for devotion, which included excerpts from spiritual writings for reflection. I basked in the spiritual wisdom of writers such as Carlo Carretto, George MacDonald, Saint Teresa of Avila, Henri Nouwen, and others.

I became particularly enamored with the writings of Carlo Carretto—so much so that I sought out his books. Without the exercise of daily devotional, I would never have discovered the depth of Christian discipleship that Carretto gave expression to in such writings as *The God Who Comes, I Sought and I Found, Letters from the Desert,* and *I, Francis.*[3] Reading Job and Shawchuck's devotional guide and then devouring Carretto's books refreshed my innermost soul. I was bathing in spiritual splendor. It energized my days.

Keeping to the practice of a daily devotional helped me clarify my thinking about everyday concerns. It brought focus on what was truly important for my ministry and my relationships: both for my own family and for my church. The entire endeavor filled my soul with peace. I faced life challenges with a greater sense of confidence that the decisions I was making were grounded in my relationship with God. I found myself anchored to something deep and abiding. The practice of a daily devotional helped me make it through the day.

I have learned over the years that a sacred space such as that oasis serves the practice of daily devotion well. It gives us a familiar space that bespeaks holiness and centers our hearts and minds on the things of God. Finding time to pray and making it a priority is the first order of business for church leaders who seek to reach their communities. When we ground our every endeavor in prayer, we can more easily avoid the pitfalls of self-reliance and keep our focus on God. I also have learned that when I fail to keep the practice, I am much more likely to get into trouble. I stray from the path that follows Jesus' way of right living. I rely instead on myself and am too easily distracted by desires that counter Jesus' way. I make poor choices based on my own earthly desires for treasures and recognition. Instead of heeding Jesus' promise that "all these things will be given to you as well" (Matt. 6:33) when striving first for God's reign, I seek to build my own kingdom. In these times I experience brokenness without a lifeline to something abiding. I am a boat without a rudder. I am disconnected to what truly matters in life and ministry. The life lesson for me is clear: stay connected to God through prayer. You will anchor yourself to the eternal. Individual church leaders will lead better when they stay connected to God through prayer and when they lead others to do the same.

E. Stanley Jones lived a life of prayer and wrote many devotional guides that blessed people around the world. It is clear from his writings that everything he did flowed from a deep prayer life. When confronted with challenges, as when he discerned his calling to focus his ministry on India's higher castes, Jones sought direction from God through prayer. He waited upon *the Voice* that would speak to his innermost being and provide clarity for a way forward.

In his book *How to Pray,* he gives us simple instructions for a meaningful prayer time:[4]

1. Set up a quiet place in the home that will serve as your personal sacred space, including symbols that will help "achieve the prayer mood."[5]

2. Relax the body and mind. Tell your body and brain that you are entering the presence of God and it is time to listen and to let go.

3. Don't be in a hurry to place your requests before God. There will be time for that.

4. Remember that a right relationship with God is the essence of prayer. Be honest with God about any barrier that prevents you from following God's direction.

5. Don't be perplexed by wandering thoughts, instead take those thoughts to God, asking for God's help in removing the distraction.

6. Cultivate the habit of prayer by keeping to a fixed time every day.

Jones said that we fool ourselves if we think we do not need a specific time and place to pray or that we can find God all the time and everywhere. I have learned this lesson the hard way, discovering that reliance on myself rather than God eats away at my confidence and separates me from the connection with God. I need to make the time and find the space to pray even when I am away from home. "If you are to find God all the time, you must find God some time," Jones wrote. "And if you are to find God everywhere, you will have to find God somewhere." He urged us to find a special prayer time and a special prayer place. Cultivating this habit will lead us on to a life of meaning and purpose.[6] If we are to embrace a missionary mindset, then we, too, need to find that sacred space where we can devote meaningful time to God.

How Church Leaders Can Lead Others to Meaningful Prayer

If we are to reach the communities in which we live, whether by starting a new church or bringing renewed vitality to an existing one, we as church leaders need to make prayer a high priority. A rich prayer life sets our focus "on things that are above" and not on "things that are on earth" (Col. 3:2). It raises questions about motive. Are our motives based on the "things that are on earth," such as adding prestige to our church? Or are they based on the desire to align ourselves with God's mission to serve as instruments of his love in the world? Prayer helps us align ourselves with what God is already doing in the neighborhood. It gets us into the "why" of what we do, moving us to reflect on our work. Why are we trying to reach our community? What difference will our mission make? Who are we trying to reach? How will our community of faith help transform the life of our town or city? What is at stake for the people who live in our midst? We are reminded of the importance of communicating clearly the essentials of the gospel: to let people know that Christ died for us and for our sins; Christ is risen so that we can have newness of life; Christ will come again in final victory to fulfill God's purposes for the world. Organizing our communal prayer life should be our first service to one another and to our mission.

Jones urged us to hold to a "prayer hour," his language for setting aside a time and place to pray. He said, "Build the habits of your life around that prayer hour. Make things fit into it, not it into things."[7] Once we have established such a habit in ourselves, we can bring others into it by leading a prayer team. We could invite four or five people together to pray, read scripture, and share the struggles and joys of living out the Christian faith on an everyday basis. The purpose of such meetings is to guide one another into a deeper spiritual experience with God and to find healing and wholeness in life.

If you are a church leader—lay or clergy—invite others to be part of your prayer team. Find two or three people with whom you can pray, claiming Jesus' promise, "For where two or three are gathered in my name, I am there among them" (Matt. 18:20). Help one another to keep the practice of daily prayer. Covenant to meet weekly face-to-face and stay in touch between times through e-mail, a private Facebook page, or other social media.[8] As a leader, your effectiveness needs to be undergirded by prayer—your own and that of others. Your team will pray for you and for one another even as you pray for them. You will help one another live out the experience of a disciple of Jesus. Lead others by example, sharing your own experiences with the practice of daily prayer—both failures and successes. Stress the importance of helping one another to hold fast to the habit of daily prayer.

The agenda for your prayer team meeting need not be complicated. Begin with a reading from the Psalms (use the psalm for the week from the Revised Common Lectionary).[9] Pray for the presence of God in your meeting. Share with one another the joys and struggles of the week and how prayer has served you through it all. Jones wrote, "Prayer is the power to get through difficulties, to be at your best, to become effective."[10] Share with one another how prayer is working in your life.

You will find people who feel uncomfortable about prayer. Perhaps they never received instruction on how to pray when they became part of a community of faith. Perhaps they were asked to pray aloud in a group and felt embarrassed and inadequate to do so. As a leader, you have an opportunity to teach the fundamentals of prayer and to help people become more at ease with it. Offer resources such as Jones's *How to Pray* to help them get started (or restarted). Find one of the many useful daily devotion resources and use it with your team as a guide.

A new church start in a Hispanic/Latino context uses the Spanish-language version of the *Upper Room* (*El Aposento Alto*) as a guide to daily prayer. They meet in small groups on Wednesdays, using the magazine as a guide for their meeting. Other groups use *Alive Now*, which includes short essays, poems, and prayers. It also includes suggestions for daily reflection and, in some issues, instructions for using *Lectio Divina*.[11]

A common practice going back many centuries, *Lectio Divina* can be used individually or in a group. The Latin term *Lectio Divina* means "divine reading." We begin with scripture, often using the Revised Common Lectionary as the guide for daily verses. We read the passage of scripture three times, each time with a different emphasis. The first time we read (or listen to another person read), we listen for a word or phrase that comes off the page and enters into our hearts. We pay attention to a word or phrase and then close our eyes and become silent as we allow the word from God to encompass our spirit.

We read the passage aloud a second time. This time we look for meaning as we ask what this passage of scripture tells us. What picture of life does it paint for us? How does the passage challenge our way of thinking? Again, we pay attention to thoughts that come to mind as we invite stillness and silence.

Finally, we read the passage a third time. This time we seek to discern how this passage of scripture is inviting us to act. What are we called to do as a result of reading this scripture? We are invited to name a concrete action step we can take *this day* to live out the promise of the passage. And we become still and silent as we wait for God's Spirit to speak to our spirits.

We need patience and persistence to practice artfully daily prayer and meditation. If we are to make prayer a high priority, we need the dedication of a long-distance runner. There are so many things that can get in the way of our prayer hour just as there are reasons not to get up and run: travel, disruptions in our daily routine, hitting the snooze button on our alarm clocks. The dedicated runner has enough patience with herself to know that there are days when it will not be possible to run. She also knows that on most days she will have the persistence to get going even if it means running in the evening instead of the morning. The apostle Paul encouraged us to foster patience: "May you be made strong with all the strength that comes from his glorious power, and may you be prepared to endure everything with patience, while joyfully giving thanks to the Father, who has enabled you to share in the inheritance of the saints in the light" (Col. 1:11-12).

Practicing *Lectio Divina* is an exercise that cultivates patience. It builds in us this virtue as we wait upon the Lord to speak to our hearts and minds and give us direction for our daily life. When I find myself too easily caught up in the hurried movement of daily life, I repeat Paul's advice to the Colossians to prepare myself to endure everything with patience, and I remind myself to slow down to the pace of *Lectio Divina*.

The missionary mindset drives us to keep our focus on God as we intercede for self, church, and community. When patience and persistence lead us to a consistent practice of our daily devotional life and we meet with others of like dedication, when we are experiencing the rhythmic balance of life and prayer, the practice ceases to be merely an exercise and begins to be part of our very selves. In this way we *become* prayer and we live closer to the apostle Paul's exhortation to "pray without ceasing" (1 Thess. 5:17). This can only happen when prayer moves from priority to predictability and from predictability to practice—a practice with which we are so comfortable that it becomes as close to us as breathing itself. The invitation then is to go beyond praying and to *be* prayer, so that it becomes a part of the self in every conversation, every new relationship, and every engagement.

Prayer can energize ministry and lead to unexpected delights. I experienced this when I had the opportunity to lead a weekend conference for Masonville United Methodist Church in New Jersey. On Saturday, a team of lay church leaders from the church went on a "prayer walk" through the neighborhood and into a nearby strip mall. The simple question, "How can we pray for you?" elicited a response from a store owner that his wife had been diagnosed with cancer. Team members prayed with him on the spot. Two weeks later the same team, who now called themselves "prayer responders," returned to the store owner, who upon seeing them through the window ran out to greet them and to thank them for the prayers for his wife. A relationship was established between the church members and the store owner.

"How can I pray for you?" This question can open many opportunities for prayer responders to leap into action. As your team becomes familiar with the collective and individual needs of the neighborhood, it also builds relationships. Keep a record of the individuals for whom you pray. Follow up on prayer requests and the people they represent.

Today, many years after living adjacent to a sacred space where I practiced a daily office, I am blessed once again to be able to pray in a splendid space. Just one floor down from my office is the Upper Room Chapel. Just entering that space evokes for me what E. Stanley Jones referred to as *the prayer mood*. A sense of the sacred emanates from the room. I can sit in the first pew and gaze upon a wood carving replica of Da Vinci's *The Last Supper*, and once again the sights and sounds provide a wonderful sense of solitude where I can refuel for ministry.

YOUR TURN:
QUESTIONS FOR REFLECTION AND DISCUSSION

1. What practice of daily prayer has worked best for you? What struggles have you had in keeping to a "prayer hour"?

2. Talk with one another about ways your community of faith can form small prayer teams.

3. As church leaders, how best can you hold one another accountable for your practice of prayer?

4. Share with one another how prayer is helping you go through this book together. (Refer to "Your Turn" at the end of chapter 1.)

3

SELF-AWARENESS
UNDERSTANDING WHO WE ARE

Know Thyself.

—PLATO

W e pray to whom it may concern." That was the part joke, part truth we murmured at the interdenominational seminary where I studied. Harvard Divinity School hosted an eclectic and ecumenical mix of students and a foretaste of the religious landscape to come in the United States. I am forever grateful for the three years I spent on that campus.

Classmates included Protestant Christians like myself as well as Jews, Roman Catholics, Hindus, Buddhists, a variety of religious expressions I had never heard of before, and those still figuring out what they believed in. What I experienced back then looks a lot like many of the communities of the United States today. Great diversity of belief and unbelief live next door to each other.

Because my classmates included people whose beliefs were quite different from my own, I learned to brace myself for criticism of things I said. Sometimes my feelings were hurt, like the time a Jewish student took me to task for the anti-Semitic lyrics of the song I sang at a chapel service. At other times I became anxious when students with an aggressive edge corrected professors for their non-gender-inclusive language. "Why are they berating that professor?" I would say to myself. I never wanted to be anti-Semitic, nor did I *not* want to be inclusive. But could the fault-finders please be a little nice about the criticism?

Upon reflection, the Jewish student was right. The lyrics *were* anti-Semitic. Did I sing those songs at summer camp? What was I teaching the children! I knew I had to take a deeper look into the songs I sang, the assumptions I made about faith and Christianity, my interpretation of scripture, my life, and my identity. In this pluralistic atmosphere, no one was going to give me any facile answers. This was not a culture that said you had to believe this or that. I had to decide if I was a United Methodist or not. I had to discover more precisely what that meant. I was forced to "know myself." This place challenged, confronted, and discomfited. The irony was that, upon deciding not to go to a seminary of my denomination, I became more riveted to my own tradition at this interdenominational school.

Divinity school forced me to gain a greater self-awareness of my religious and spiritual values, what I could affirm and what I could not affirm. The faith of my father and mother and family was something to cling to. I ended up affirming my faith tradition as a United Methodist. I decided that United Methodism was my home and that I would remain in it even as I was exposed to so many other expressions of faith. Methodism was born as a movement that extended beyond the confines of a single denomination (the Church of England). It never intended to be a separate denomination. It sought to include others in living the faith in a real, day-to-day way. In the face of so many ways to believe in God or not believe in anything, I chose the church I had grown up in.

Self-awareness is key to a missionary mindset. E. Stanley Jones was keenly aware of his own religious tradition. He learned to take a step back from his tradition and listen to those who came from a different tribe. He showed that he respected them and valued them by laying aside his own claims to the truth of Christianity and inviting them to a roundtable of discussion where they could share the truth as they had come to know it. He offered a venue of open dialogue and encouraged honest and civil interaction as people from differing faith perspectives and those with no faith perspective at all had a chance to be in conversation with one another. One of the lessons we can learn from the mission ministry of Jones is to love and respect our neighbors and all of their diversity.

Self-awareness can undergird our efforts to reach out to new people as we take part in new church planting or the revitalization of existing churches. We can draw upon self-awareness tools that can help us understand better our personality type and how we differ from other personality types. We can group these tools under the rubric of "My Personality Type." We can also reflect deeply on our own stories, reminding ourselves how family dynamics together with our neighborhood environment have shaped who we are. These fall under the heading of "My Story." A third methodology for understanding ourselves better individually is by identifying "My Default Culture." We explored this in the introduction. Recall that a "default culture" is firmly embedded in who we are. As we seek to gain a missionary mindset in the new area of ministry, we recognize our own default culture and work to go beyond it to embrace the culture of those with whom we are sharing the gospel of Jesus Christ. Becoming clear about our default culture in anticipation of getting to know a culture not our own is key to learning how to build a bridge of love and understanding between ourselves and those with whom we want to share the gospel of Jesus. In this chapter we will explore each of these groupings as we attempt to gain clarity about ourselves so that we can overcome any lack of affinity with the population group we are trying to reach.

MY PERSONALITY TYPE

For years now those of us who have worked in new church development have required that potential planters of communities of faith participate in a self-assessment process. The practice makes sense not only for new church planters, but also for leaders of existing churches. Instruments that help us know ourselves better will help us gain confidence in accentuating our strengths and at the same time recognize the value and importance of surrounding ourselves with people whose personality type complements our own. If we want to be intentional about reaching out to cultures not our own, it will be important to self-assess and know our own personality style.

Many assessment tools for exploring personality type are available, and you can explore them on the Internet. We focus on two: the DiSC Profile and the Myers-Briggs Type Indicator.[1] In addition to these profiles, we can use other tools to help us discover how we deal with conflict, what our spirituality style is, and other aspects of our personality, thus assessing and building cross-cultural competence. In the appendix you will find references to websites and written resources to access these tools.

DiSC is an acronym for *Dominance, Influence, Steadiness,* and *Conscientiousness.* These are the four behavioral traits measured by the inventory. Discovering our "DiSC profile" helps us know our default behavioral styles as we relate to others in the workplace, as we lead others, and as we manage situations and environments. Based on the original work of William Mouton Marston, DiSC is now in its third generation of use. Online survey tools can generate instant feedback regarding our particular personality style.[2]

My DiSC profile reveals that I have a high D personality style, with medium S and C, and low I. This means that I tend to take charge, get the task done. I don't do much to win friends and influence people. I am more the type to stay the course and get to the finish line. I can be more effective in my work if I surround myself with people whose personality types include the higher "I." These are the influencers, who draw people naturally to themselves. They tend to be extroverts who win people on the strength of their personality. They easily strike up a conversation. Others find them winsome and want to follow their lead.

I have also taken the Myers-Briggs Type Indicator (MBTI). Our work team wanted to learn the personality type of each of its members so we could understand each other and work together better. It identifies four main preference pairs:

- Extroversion (E) and Introversion (I): Do we focus more on the outer world or our own inner world?
- Sensing (S) and Intuition (N): Do we prefer to focus on the information we can gather with our senses, or would we rather interpret and add meaning to the information we gather?
- Thinking (T) and Feeling (F): When we make decisions, do we prefer to look at logic and consistency or at the people and circumstances of the situation?
- Judging (J) and Perceiving (P): In the way we perceive our world, do we prefer to make decisions (using our thinking

or feeling function) or to stay open to new information and options (using our sensing or intuiting function)?

I learned that my personality type pointed to introversion, intuition, feeling, and judging.

Types are not right or wrong. Knowledge of them simply helps us understand ourselves. When we take this assessment along with fellow workers or team members, we gain greater insight into why we and others behave the way we do. When I learned my own type, I also learned that others might perceive me in ways I don't like. Others sometimes perceive my inclination to introversion as "aloofness." I don't want to appear aloof to others. Because of my personality type, I need to be aware that I may come off that way and seek to mitigate it as best I can. Said Isabel Briggs Myers, "When people differ, a knowledge of type lessens friction and eases strain. In addition, it reveals the value of differences. No one has to be good at everything."[3]

A young pastor starting a new church in a large city used personality tools not only to help him understand himself, but also to seek complementary personalities for his launch team. On the DiSC profile, he discovered that he was more of the conscientious type. His Myers-Briggs Type Indicator pointed to his introversion. He knew that he needed to surround himself with influencers and extroverts. He used the inventories to help his team work together and to guide in the identification of leaders.

Third-party tools help us gain greater self-awareness and also help us understand how we approach life and opportunities in ways that are different from people who have other personality types. When we understand a particular tool well and we invite our team to take the same inventory, we can better understand each other and the dynamics of teamwork that can help us achieve the results we hope for in our work.

MY STORY

I am also invited to know my story and how it is larger than my call-to-ministry story. I have had the privilege to administer a program where younger clergy learn at the feet of experienced pastors. Each year when we bring together a new cohort of what we call the "High Impact Church Planting Residents," we spend time sharing our stories. I am always thankful to God for the heartfelt disclosing that goes on. By sharing our stories with one another, we bring ourselves closer and are able to experience a sense of community. By articulating aloud our own stories to others, we become more self-aware. The exercise forces us to reflect on who we are. Storytelling clarifies our self-awareness. It fuels loyalty to community. How can we possibly tell the story of our faith in Jesus if we have not first reflected on how *we* have been impacted by that story?

One year a participant shared how frustrating and dehumanizing the ordination process had been for her. She said that she was about to give up on the church until the residency program offered a way forward. She had not grown up in the church and in fact had a difficult childhood that included an abusive father and a drug-addicted mother. Because she had not grown up in the church, she did not know the common vocabulary that churched people often take for granted. Those who were part of the process for interviewing her for ordination found it difficult to connect with her. At times she felt humiliated and misunderstood. She was attempting to follow a call for ministry and couldn't quite articulate that call in a way her interviewers could understand. The residency offered her a year to learn under the tutelage of an experienced church planter, who helped her work through her feelings and at the same time gain practical knowledge about how to do ministry.

As a missionary, I was given the opportunity to reflect on my own faith story. When I lived and served in Rosario, Argentina, my supervising minister, Hugo Urcola, assigned me the task of developing an evangelization initiative for our region. I didn't have any experience in this kind of endeavor and didn't know where to start. My seminary training had not prepared me to involve myself in an evangelization initiative. That is, there were no courses offered in faith sharing or evangelism or anything of the like. Yet, seminary did teach me to think through a challenge and to approach it from a biblical-theological perspective. I began reading scriptures that focused on sharing the gospel. Hugo Urcola's assignment led me to the writings of E. Stanley Jones. I began asking myself basic questions, such as, what is the gospel? Why would it be important that others who are not part of our church or any church come into a relationship with Jesus?

I knew I needed the help of others to initiate a new program of evangelism for the region. I needed the help of fellow pastors as well as laity. I sensed that they, too, needed to struggle with answers to basic questions about the gospel and relating to others just as I had. We formed an evangelism team and together we thought through these questions. We knew that we had to discover for ourselves what the essentials of the gospel were so that we could communicate clearly why faith in Christ is important and why it makes a difference for a person's life.

We began to articulate a methodology that included three simple steps: listen, respond, and invite. We *listened* to the stories of the people we encountered. We wanted to be sure we understood their needs, their hopes, and their concerns. We *responded* to their stories by sharing scriptural passages that spoke to their needs. We *invited* people to take the next logical step toward faith. Sometimes it was a simple invitation to pray. If the person we encountered seemed ready to embrace a deeper commitment to

God, we would invite that individual to follow Jesus as his or her leader of life.

Many years have passed since we held those first meetings that formed an evangelization team. Today, in addition to the steps of listening, responding, and inviting, I would want to transmit clarity about what the gospel is. I would want to invite people to affirm what Christ has done for us through his death, resurrection, and by his promised coming. I would affirm the essential gospel message that Christ has died; Christ is risen; Christ will come again.

Those who responded to the call for a team were mostly younger adults. They were eager to explore their faith more deeply and resonated with the idea of learning more about what their faith meant to them so they could be more confident sharing faith with others. We met together for a retreat and decided that this team would serve the entire region and help churches evangelize in a way that made sense for their particular community. After reflecting on several scripture passages on the first night of our retreat, we asked each participant to think through his or her own story. Team members were each to come prepared the next morning with a one-page description of how they came to be part of a community of faith that followed Jesus and what it meant to them.

We spent the morning listening to one another's stories and then finding the similarities and differences among them. We learned that each story has value and import not only for the person sharing but also for those hearing. We learned something about each other and how the gospel impacts people in different ways. Most of the participants had grown up in the church. Their parents had been members and had simply brought them along. They had each arrived at a point in their faith journey when belonging to a community of faith was not just something their parents wanted for them, but that they wanted for themselves.

Some of the participants had no church background and had come to faith in Jesus as adults. Things that others who had grown up in the church took for granted were unknown or new for them. We spoke about how important it would be for each of us to know both our own story and the stories of others as we talked with new people. We might remember something in a team member's story that would resonate with a person we are talking to. For instance, if someone we visited had little or no exposure to church life, we could share the story of Alicia, who came to church as an adult. We could recount Alicia's testimony of needing direction and purpose for her life and finding it when she met up with other younger adults who met for prayer and recreation on Sunday nights. When we met with someone who had grown up in the church but had drifted away, we shared the story of Isabel, who had left her parents' faith tradition entirely while living in another city, only to find herself drawn back to the church through the love and companionship of a friend.

During that weekend we outlined a plan of action for visiting an existing church in the region. We would travel to that town on a Friday and conduct a workshop with members of the local church. There we would go through some of the same exercises we had done on the retreat. On Saturday, we would pair local church people with members of our team and visit people who had been associated in one way or another with the local church. We called ourselves "fishers." We never made "cold calls" on people. The local church always asked people first if we could make the visits. That kind of strategy worked in Arroyo Seco, although it may not work in your context. Ironically, the translation of the name of the town we first visited was called "Dry Stream" (*Arroyo Seco*). Despite its name, we managed to catch some new people for the local church.

We always left each conversation, each home visited, with an invitation to attend a gathering that would include music and a movie that same evening. Then, we gathered back at the church to debrief our visits. Invariably we talked of how the people we'd visited had so much to teach us and how thankful we were for the opportunity to get to know them. I was particularly blessed to get to know Brother Amérigo Suarez. Amérigo was one of the lay leaders of the local church in Arroyo Seco. I will share more about Amérigo and his unique lay ministry when we address humility in chapter 5.

Because we had rehearsed our stories during the retreat, we were more readily able to share stories in the homes of people we visited once we traveled to churches in the region. It was the telling of our stories that helped us gain greater self-awareness. We were able to articulate our own faith stories. At the same time, we gained appreciation and respect for other people's stories. We affirmed that there are different ways to come to faith in Jesus.

MY DEFAULT CULTURE

We enrich self-knowledge by knowing our personality types, and we are better able to share the good news when we have articulated our particular faith stories. Knowledge of our default culture also makes us more effective witnesses for our faith. The experience of Iosmar Alvarez, a Cuban American church planter in Kentucky, helps us understand the dynamic of self-awareness and default culture.

Alvarez spoke to a gathering of judicatory staff responsible for new church development and congregational transformation about challenges of Hispanic/Latino ministry in the United States. The meeting took place in Oklahoma City, Oklahoma, in May of 2015. One of the points he made was the importance of leaving behind one's culture of origin in order to connect with the culture of other people. "If I try to start a church that is Cuban," he said, "I am lost!

There are not enough fellow Cubans living in Kentucky. I have to learn about the culture and music of Puerto Ricans, Mexicans, Central Americans."

Iosmar's point was that he had to separate himself from his "default culture" in order to embrace other Hispanic/Latinos from other countries and contexts. Furthermore, Alvarez underscored the importance of understanding different generations within the Hispanic/Latino community. "Not all persons of Hispanic/Latino descent speak Spanish," he emphasized. He talked of the importance of understanding the "Joshua" generation (first-generation immigrants) and the "Joseph" generation (second generation). Children growing up in the United States experience reality differently than their parents who grew up in the mother country. These differing cultural dynamics can lead to tensions and miscommunication. The parent generation expects children to respond to them as they had responded to their parents in the "old country." Living in a new culture changes that.

I saw these generational dynamics at play among Korean Americans in New Jersey. Pastors distinguished among the differing forces at work of first-generation Koreans (those who immigrated from Korea) the *1.5 generation* (those who were born in Korea but came to the United States in childhood) and the *2.0 generation* (those born in the United States). In the Korean American community, as well as other new immigrant communities (Chinese, Philippine, Southeast Asian, among others), a first-generation pastor needs to cultivate a self-awareness of his own perspective on life and suspend his default tendencies in order to connect with subsequent generations. For instance, first-generation Korean parents in New Jersey expected their children to defer to their judgment and decision making regarding matters of church life. That expectation was part of their inheritance from Korean culture. The 1.5- and 2.0-generation children, now grown up and used to making their own decisions in the United States (many had become doctors and lawyers and successful in business), resented such interference. A first-generation pastor, fully aware of these dynamics and naturally inclined to default to the Korean parents' point of view, had to navigate the tensions between the generations. To be pastor to the younger generations, he had to suspend his default in order to help the younger generation find their place in the life of the church.

As the United States becomes more and more diverse, gaining clarity about my own culture becomes even more important. As a white, English-speaking person in the United States, I have had a privileged position in this country. I take for granted certain perspectives and understandings as part of the dominant culture of the land. I experienced this firsthand when I served a multiethnic church in New Jersey. When I arrived as pastor in 1987, the congregation included individuals born in twenty-two nations, incorporating the Caribbean, West Africa, India, and East Asia as well as African Americans and Anglo-American people. I learned that as a white Anglo, I embodied the dominant culture many immigrants aspired to join. I had a built-in advantage over colleague nonwhite pastors in this context. Many immigrant peoples wanted to identify with what I was. The challenge for me was to not allow my privilege to oppress people. I worked hard to celebrate the differing perspectives of cultures and to affirm the music, leadership styles, and characteristics of the myriad cultures that were part of the mix of the church.

For example, our young African American, Afro-Caribbean, and West African women formed a liturgical dance troupe for worship, and we wanted to celebrate their spiritual expression. Our Indian Asian members explained to me that seeing young women in leotards in church went against their own cultural understandings. Leaders of our Indian Asian constituency sat down with me to talk about their uneasiness with the dance troupe (we called them "Spirit Dancers"). Allowing for conversation about the conflict led us to consensus. The Indian Asians wanted to affirm the young African-descendant women's artistic expression. At the same time they realized that their objection to leotards in the chancel harked back to certain aspects of their Indian culture that they disliked. To their credit, the Indian Asian members, who greatly valued being part of a multiethnic congregation, learned to suspend their default-culture understandings in order to be open to something new. They were able to go beyond their default to embrace the larger community.

Eric H. F. Law, founder and director of the Kaleidoscope Institute,[4] has helped churches navigate sensitivities in a multiethnic context. His ministry focuses "on how Christians can follow Christ's call to seek and serve Christ in every person and respect the dignity of every human being."[5] The Kaleidoscope Institute and the books that Law wrote are helpful resources for the Christian leader who seeks to reach his or her community with the gospel of Jesus Christ. Law invites us to understand the dynamics of our own culture so we can include people from other cultures in conversation and level the playing field for more openness to one another and the meaning behind our words. He has coined the phrase "dialogue by mutual invitation," which becomes a means to get to know one another better and to build the relationship.[6] For example, Americans are known for their outspokenness. People from other cultures may appear to be quiet. In fact, they might have something to say in a group but be reluctant to do so until invited. Thus, it is important, knowing that our own culture may have a proclivity for outspokenness, to be proactive and invite others into the conversation. In this way we act on an understanding of ourselves and on the inclusion of others.

As a multiethnic staff team in New Jersey, we drew from Law's "dialogue by mutual invitation" to afford everyone an equal chance to speak.[7] We would hold on to a bean bag while speaking and then, when finished, pass (or throw) the bag to another member of the group while saying the person's name and inviting him or her to share. One could always choose to "pass" and then invite someone else to speak. This practice kept our default culture in check and allowed us to be more intentional about listening to one another. Self-awareness affords us insight into who we are so that we are conscientious enough to step back from time to time to allow others to step forward.

It is difficult to separate ourselves from our default culture. At times, we will inevitably fall back on a way of thinking we were taught as children or a way of behaving we saw modeled in our families. Sometimes when we feel challenged or on the defensive, our natural tendency will be to return to our default culture. We do so out of a need for self-preservation. When under pressure in a group situation or when colleagues aggressively tease us, we might say something stupid that we regret. When cornered, we push the "reset" button and return to our default culture. Perhaps our true colors have come out. We feel humiliation. This kind of situation leads to hurt feelings, broken relationships, and awkwardness.

Self-awareness can help us recognize the difference between the individuals we were taught to be (default) and the person we are trying to become in Christ. It can also help us avoid losing our cool and behaving in ways we later regret. We can be honest about what we are feeling as we become aware. "I am ticked off right now and don't want to say something I'll regret. Please give me some space before we go on."

When we hold conversations with each other and attempt to build relationships as a community that includes people of a different culture, we get closer to a "missionary mindset" that at once allows us to know our default culture and listens to the other without judgment. These cross-cultural conversations can occur among ethnicities, races, generations, religious perspectives, and skeptics.

Self-awareness helps the church leader to navigate the waters between what has been and what can be. Knowing where we have been and the cultural trappings that have shaped us offers us the first step toward being open to other perspectives, other cultural partialities. We create breathing room between our own cultural default system and other cultural systems. We then look for opportunities to better understand the people we are trying to reach and to learn of their cultural background. We are intentional about finding ways to make a bridge of love and understanding between who we are and who they are. We open the possibility and the promise of connecting to new people.

YOUR TURN:
QUESTIONS FOR REFLECTION AND DISCUSSION

1. Why is it important to know ourselves as we seek to reach people in our community?

2. What different cultures and religious traditions are present in the community in which you serve?

3. Share your experience with personality inventories and how they have helped you understand yourself and your default culture.

4. How does self-awareness prepare us for interacting in a multiethnic environment?

4

LISTENING
TAKING THE RISK TO UNDERSTAND

Ears to hear and eyes to see—
the LORD made them both.

—PROVERBS 20:12 CEB

I n the first months of learning to speak Spanish, I had to intensify my listening skills. I strained to understand what was being said. Listening was an activity of both auditory attention and comprehension. I couldn't begin to comprehend until I correctly interpreted the sounds I heard. In the beginning, my mind couldn't process fast enough. I kept asking others to repeat what they said. Sometimes they would speak louder, as if the problem were auditory alone. I made lots of mistakes. Fortunately, my Argentine friends had a keen sense of humor and lots of patience to put up with me.

One summer afternoon just three months after arriving in the country, Bishop Gattinoni's daughter, Marta, invited us on an outing in her outboard motor boat through the Paraná delta. Though

Marta spoke English fluently, she spoke Spanish that day to help us learn the language. Admiring the boat, I attempted to ask, in Spanish, if the trim was made of wood (*madera*). However, I confused the word for wood with the street word for feces. Marta laughed and told me what I had said and taught me the distinction between *madera* and *mie*da*.

Learning a new language calls for a sense of humor and a good dose of self-deprecation. I had to learn to laugh at myself and be willing to look foolish to advance my understanding and skill. It gave me a great appreciation for the millions of immigrants who come to the United States and have to learn English.

Listening begins with attentiveness to the other. As the book of Proverbs says, we have ears to *hear*! To hear someone truly, we need to pay attention. I must be ready to *so* value what the other person says that I hang on every word to understand fully both the meaning of the words and their underlying import. I purposely direct attention away from myself and toward the other. I "say" through actions that what *you* are saying is the most important, most valuable piece of information in the world.

Do you not feel valued and honored when someone truly listens to you and you know he or she is listening? It makes me feel important when another person listens to me. Knowing how I feel when others listen to me, when I fail to listen, I make the other person feel devalued and unimportant. I contribute to his or her lack of self-esteem. It is demeaning. When I realize that I have not listened, I feel bad because I know that listening is much more than hearing the words. It is about valuing the person.

Sometimes when I converse with people a generation or two younger than I am, I need to employ the same skills and intensity as when I was learning Spanish. We are both speaking English, yet I need to pay close attention to understand the meaning of words spoken and their underlying significance. And sometimes

I need to admit that I don't understand—that I need clarification or explanation. "Help me understand what you are saying," is a favorite phrase I employ when speaking with younger people. Sometimes I don't understand the meaning of the words, as when someone uses a technical computer term with which I am not yet familiar or refers to popular culture.

These are challenging times for communication—at least for me. So, let's break down some important skills for listening in an attempt to foster clear communication for the sake of reaching communities with the good news of Jesus Christ. In addition to requiring a sense of humor and attentiveness, good listening involves *presence* and *promise*.

PRESENCE

One of the five vows that United Methodists take upon joining a local church is to uphold the church through their *presence*. "Presence," according to *Webster's Third New International Dictionary*, refers to "the state of being in one place and not elsewhere . . . the part of space within one's ken, call, or influence."[1] Good listening skills require such presence. We talk of being present to another person or group. Such *presence* is vital when entering into new missional territory. We listen deeply to the people who live in our neighborhoods. We look for intentional ways to deepen our understanding of the problems and the possibilities for this area. We do so by being present to others in such a way that they are valued. When we are truly present to people in a new missional area through listening and understanding, we build relationships of trust and have the opportunity to gain a hearing from them.

My default mode of interaction is quiet. I was the kid who seldom raised his hand in class. As I mentioned in the last chapter, the personality tests always scored me as an introvert. Sometimes my quietness has been interpreted as aloofness. Giving the impression of being aloof is the opposite of what good listening calls for. I have had to work extra hard as a church leader to overcome my natural tendencies (my default) to quietness. But I can demonstrate I am attending to another in ways other than speaking. A good question I have had to ask myself in interactions is: "Am I truly present to others?" I need to show others that I am listening through body language, eye contact, tone of voice, posture, and by feeding back to the person or persons with whom I am talking a summary of what I have heard and then asking if I have heard accurately.

The use of smartphones during meetings drives me crazy and seems to go against not only my own sense of decorum but the dictionary definition of presence. Picture five people around a table, discussing a topic, and two participants are simultaneously looking at their phones. They are each texting to someone on their phones or reading e-mail, yet supposedly participating in the meeting at the same time. I prefer "the state of being in one place and not elsewhere" and giving one's undivided attention in a discussion. I am often amazed when those who are texting pretend not to have lost a beat. In truth, they are not fully participating in the meeting. They are not present. Moreover, Sherry Turkle, in a *New York Times* article, cites research indicating "that when two people are talking, the mere presence of a phone on a table between them or in the periphery of their vision changes both what they talk about and the degree of connection they feel."[2] We cannot be present to another when our phones are in the way.

Presence implies full listening. I am not only hearing what is said; I am paying attention to the story and the players and the context. I am "reading" the situation so that my understanding can go deep. If I am unsure that I am reading correctly what is going on, I ask for clarification. More than being proximate to another, being *present* communicates full awareness of the other's story.

E. Stanley Jones became present to people of other religions in India when he created a forum for listening to one another through the roundtable. His goal was to allow others to give Christianity a fair hearing. Jones trusted that once people opened themselves to one another in a sympathetic atmosphere, they would be able to evaluate the efficacy of their belief system. He advocated for an attitude that at once appreciated other religions (or the life view of "skeptics" who professed no religion at all) as well as appraised them. The bottom line for Jones was whether your belief system works. Does it help you live a better life? Are you a better person because of it? Do you make good, ethical choices in life? Are you contributing to the betterment of humankind? Jones was convinced that the truth of Christ, who stands over and above even Christianity itself, would draw people to the Christian message of the kingdom. Jones himself did not need to coerce. He only had to offer the conditions whereby Christ could gain entrance. Jones learned the importance of listening to others and practicing authentic openness to others' beliefs. By deeply listening to the roundtable discussions that included Buddhists, Muslims, Hindus, Christians, and skeptics, he opened himself to their ideas, their belief systems. Rarely do we permit ourselves to understand a different point of view, especially when that point of view can challenge our own way of thinking about our faith. Usually, we human beings react to others first, rather than listen. We evaluate what they are saying. We judge whether or not what they say is true. We seldom seek to truly understand the other person, which we can do only when we suspend any tendency to evaluate or judge and, instead, listen. If I let myself truly understand another person, that understanding might change me. Understanding another is risky business.

I take the risk to be vulnerable enough to the person with whom I am present that I may come to accept her belief, her opinion, or her theology. As the R.E.M. song goes, I risk losing my religion. If that religion or belief system has anchored my life, I give up a significant aspect of my identity. The risk of being present to another and listening deeply may change me in ways too scary to contemplate. E. Stanley Jones was able to risk such listening and such honest, open exchange with people who held other beliefs because he was anchored in an even deeper trust in God. We are not all so grounded in our faith, and thus the vulnerability and risk involved with listening opens us to the unknown and the possibility of change.

A young woman who had grown up Roman Catholic began attending the United Methodist church I served in New Jersey. She was attracted to the way we worshipped, with our eclectic mix of music from different parts of the world and simple liturgy, and she asked to talk with me about her faith. She was genuinely perplexed. At our church, she had been exposed to a different belief system and way of relating to God, and she confessed to me that it was making her feel anxious. She explained how she had grown up as an active member of the Roman Catholic Church and was worried that she could be making the wrong decision if she were to join our church. I sensed that it was too risky for her, at least at this stage in her life, to make the move from her old belief system to a new one, so I asked her if she had shared these concerns with a priest. She immediately brightened, surprised that I would suggest this.

"Talk to your priest," I said. "Let him know what you are struggling with. We welcome you here anytime. You will always be welcome. But we want you to come with a sense that this is the right thing for you to do."

She did talk to her priest and let me know later that because of that conversation, she was able to reconnect to her church roots.

She was thankful that I'd listened and that by inviting her to talk to her priest, I'd given her permission to sort out her beliefs.

For this young woman, the risk of opening herself to a new belief system proved too much to handle. Sometimes, though, through the exchange that comes with listening deeply, I gain greater understanding of what God is calling me to be. I can gain a new awareness of life that helps me be a better person.

Through listening, I risk giving up what has always been mine even as I seek to understand others. People will know that our listening is sincere and authentic when we are truly present to them and become vulnerable in our conversation. We risk leading ourselves to change the way we think, and through our example, we model for others a similar transparency and openness to change.

Let me try to illustrate. While serving as a missionary and living in the small city of Dolores, Argentina, I befriended a pair of Mormon missionaries. A young missionary from California was paired with a Mormon from Paraguay, and they were assigned to Dolores. I met them on the street one day while walking in town. They were easily identifiable with their dark pants, white shirts, ties, and name badges. I introduced myself to them and invited them to stop by our parsonage. We enjoyed several pleasant visits in which we talked about life in Argentina as foreigners and things we missed about our home countries.

Knowing that they were far from their respective countries, after several visits, we invited them to our house for a home-cooked meal and fellowship. The Paraguayan Mormon became interested in Methodism. He had not heard of it before, and because of the relationship we struck, he began to ask questions to satisfy his curiosity. In a small way, we had offered a space for honest exchange about our respective faith traditions. We were equally curious about his faith story and how he had come to be a Mormon and to give up two years to serve as a missionary. We noticed that the California Mormon seemed uneasy about the conversation, as if we were deviating from a rule by listening to one another and sharing with one another stories of our faith traditions.

We were saddened to learn that a week after our shared meal, the team was reassigned to another city in Argentina. We wondered if the act of listening and sharing with one another had been too risky for the parameters of that particular Mormon mission. Becoming vulnerable to one another through listening and understanding can indeed be threatening. If we want to avoid any chance of change, we had best shut down that possibility by *not* listening, *not* trying to understand. By avoiding the chance for change, though, we can miss out on the gift of sharing our common humanity and reducing the barriers that separate us. Providing a safe environment where this can happen, as E. Stanley Jones did at the roundtable, creates at once both an opportunity and a risk. We can open ourselves to new understandings about life and faith. We can stretch the boundaries of long-held beliefs from our own faith tradition. We risk calling into question some long-held beliefs. This is the risk of listening deeply and being present to another.

The gospel of John shows us how Jesus became present to a Samaritan woman at the well (John 4:6-30) and how he elicited from her such a response when he purposely broke the rules of his default culture by speaking to her. Tradition held that Jews should not speak to Samaritans. Even more so, a Jewish man should not speak to a woman in public. Jesus broke these taboos to enter into a relationship with a woman and reveal himself to her so that she might experience life more abundantly. Jesus' understanding of the kingdom of God included people heretofore living at the periphery of community. To bring them into the kingdom, Jesus was truly *present* to them.

John sets the stage for the encounter by having the disciples go off to town to get food, leaving Jesus alone by Jacob's well in Samaria. A woman comes to draw water at noon and the plot thickens: a Jewish man and a Samaritan woman interact, violating a taboo. The woman comes to the well at noon because she does not want to be seen by others. Other women have already come to fetch the water and by noon are laying out the food for the midday meal. She hopes to get the water unnoticed.

Instead of defaulting to the traditional mores of the day, which would have prevented any interaction at all, Jesus breaks the rules by asking for a drink of water. Jews and Samaritans were not to have any kind of contact. If they did have physical contact, even as innocently as brushing up against one another at the market, a Jew would need to go to a priest to be cleansed ritually, for he had become defiled. By asking for water, Jesus becomes *present* to the Samaritan. Noticing he does not have a cup, the woman realizes that by asking for water, Jesus asks to drink from her vessel. Taboo would dictate no interaction, no touching, and no recognition. Jesus instead indicates, "I will put my lips to the same vessel to which you put your lips."

He has her attention.

He was *present* to her. The conversation goes deeper, and the relationship grows stronger by the second. There is a rich interchange of dialogue. Jesus seizes an opportunity to help the woman understand something new about herself and her faith. "If you knew the gift of God, and who it is that is saying to you, 'Give me a drink,' you would have asked him, and he would have given you living water" (John 4:10). If I were staging this scene in a drama, I would direct the Samaritan to look around as if to make sure that no one was watching this illicit, taboo-breaking conversation unfold, lest she get into trouble, more trouble than she already is in. She says, "Sir, you have no bucket, and the well is deep. Where do you get that living water?" (v. 11).

The conversation goes back and forth. The woman shows intelligence and increasing understanding. She wonders if the living water Jesus offers could be greater than the water she drew from the well established by Jacob. By keeping the dialogue going and by asking questions, the Samaritan woman helps move the conversation from the superficial to the spiritual. Jesus is able to interact with her and take her to new levels of understanding. He goes way beyond the dictates of his default culture and embraces the moment as the opportune time to be truly present unto her. This is an example of deep listening. The woman asks for the water Jesus offers.

For years I misinterpreted what comes next in the conversation. Jesus asks the woman to go get her husband, and she responds by saying, "I have none." He, in turn, says she is right, because the one with whom she is living is not her husband. I long misinterpreted this piece of the conversation as a revelation of her sin: having multiple partners. Yet, I have learned, by careful reading of Jewish sources, that in Jesus' day, with few exceptions, it was only the man who could transact a writ of divorce.[3] The fact that she had had five husbands would most likely have meant that she was unable to have children; therefore, one by one her husbands had cast her out. Jesus had spoken to the core of her pain and her humiliation by affirming that what she said was true.

Again, the conversation is taken to a spiritual level. Suddenly the woman sees there's more to Jesus than meets the eye.

> The woman said to him, "Sir, I see that you are a prophet. Our ancestors worshiped on this mountain, but you say that the place where people must worship is in Jerusalem. . . . I know that Messiah is coming" (who is called Christ). "When he comes, he will proclaim all things to us." Jesus said to her, "I am he, the one who is speaking to you." (John 4:19-20, 25-26)

Because Jesus was willing to go beyond his default culture and become present to this woman, the conversation that began between a Jewish man and Samaritan woman is now elevated to a conversation about the Messiah. She is the one who mentions "Messiah," thereby affirming that Jesus has listened deeply to her pain and position in life. And then Jesus does something here in this passage that does not happen anywhere else in the Bible. When talk turns to Messiah, he says, "I am he." This is the only place in the Bible where Jesus reveals himself as Messiah to another person. And who is the recipient of such news? A woman scorned and humiliated from an *ethné* that is different. The kingdom, Jesus demonstrates, includes such people. We would do well to follow Jesus' lead to be *present* to others and thereby extend a radical invitation to be part of the kingdom.

Jesus offered the Samaritan woman a different kind of understanding that brought wholeness to her brokenness and lifted her out of the embarrassment of humiliation into a life with new meaning and a new purpose. Only now she can do nothing else but drop everything to tell others of the man "who told me everything I had ever done" (v. 29), to invite others to hear him as well, and to enter into a relationship with him. What revelations will come when we are present to others through deep listening!

PROMISE

New churches that want to build trust and love in a community can learn a lesson from the deep listening that Jesus demonstrated in his encounter with the woman at the well. Currently I belong to a launch team for a new church start in East Nashville that seeks to listen deeply to its neighbors. We met children and their parents at "Ice Cream in the Park"; we tailgated next to townsfolk at the local high school football game; we sponsored a community "Fun Night" open to all. Individual team members were encouraged to join local gyms and neighborhood associations, and to volunteer at school. Being present is a fruit of listening because it gets us into many different areas of the community where we can build relationships and learn what is happening.

Our team also values what I have come to know as the *promise* of listening as we discern what God and the people of East Nashville want our church to be. By "promise" I refer to aspirations of the people for whom they want to be. If we as a launch team want to make a difference in the lives of people in East Nashville, our listening needs to bear fruit in action—action that meets people at their point of need. We spend time walking the neighborhood, hearing people's stories, asking questions. Through listening, we gain clarity about their hurts and hunger, their hopes and high goals. Listening helps us see life from the perspective of the people living in the neighborhood. Learning to listen deeply to the people in our mission area allows us entry into the promise of this community. The East Nashville neighborhood where the Reverend Erica Allen[4] envisions planting the East Bank Church (named for the east bank of the Cumberland River, across the bridge from downtown) is a mix of poverty and gentrification. Residents include whites and blacks and Latinos and immigrants from the Middle East and Africa. It is a microcosm of the contradictions and the confidence of a growing city. Our launch team meetings are times of visioning, reflection, prayer, and communion. Reverend Allen also gives us assignments. She sends us into the neighborhood to meet others and to listen to their stories. "Where will you go in the coming weeks?" she asks. How can we be the hands and feet of Jesus in this neighborhood? How can we imbue our interactions with the spirit and essence of the One we have chosen to follow? How can we expect to enter deeply into the conversations of the neighborhood if we don't involve them in conversation? We wrestle with these questions as a team, so we can gain clarity as to our purpose for forming Christian community here. Out of our conversations as a team and in light of our listening deeply to our neighbors, we glimpse the *promise* of East Nashville.

We gain a feel for the possibilities and the problems facing this part of the city. We become familiar with the area of the neighborhood where houses are boarded up, and we begin to ask questions. We notice the old gas station that has been converted into an upscale coffee house. We see the signs announcing demolition of old buildings and the photos of new dwellings to come. We interact with people along the way, and we ask more and more questions. We talk to shop owners and real estate agents and police officers on the beat because we want to learn.

We ask questions that invite responses and that do not put people on the defensive. For instance, we ask, "What do you see happening in this neighborhood?" Or, "How has this part of Nashville changed for you?" We avoid questions that start with "why," for they often put people on the defensive.

Being honest and transparent on such neighborhood walks is important. We want to gain credibility and respect, so we can build relationships that endure. People are naturally suspect of wanderers who ask questions. Sometimes I start by saying, "I'm new to the neighborhood, and I'm trying to get a feel for it. May I ask you a few questions?" Some people will be put off immediately and say they are too busy. Others oblige. Once the ice has been broken and we have chatted a bit, I share that I am a minister and part of a team of people who are starting a new community of faith. We are walking about the neighborhood, trying to get to know it better. We are trying to learn about its needs, and we are eager to hear the stories of the people who live there.

Listening demands that we are present to the people whom we want to reach with the message of the gospel. The fruit of good listening creates promise for the future for all who live in the community. When people see the connection between our listening, their needs, and actions that make lives better, our effort—as a new church plant or as an existing church reengaging its community— brings hope. We become instruments for God's transformation of the world.

YOUR TURN:
QUESTIONS FOR REFLECTION AND DISCUSSION

1. Share experiences of times when you have felt listened to.

2. What steps can your church take to proactively listen to the needs of its community?

3. Discuss how Jesus gives us an example of being present in the story of the woman at the well.

4. How would you describe the "aspirations" of your community? How can your church be part of the promise of the community?

5

HUMILITY

LOOKING TO LIFT OTHERS

*"All who exalt themselves will be humbled, and
all who humble themselves will be exalted."*
—MATTHEW 23:12

I n the late 1990s and 2000s, my friend and former supervisor,
Hugo Urcola, was appointed to serve as pastor of the First
Methodist Church in Buenos Aires. He was also elected superintendent for the metropolitan region. First Methodist is located in
the heart of the city, two blocks south of a major pedestrian street
where shops and restaurants beckon tourists and locals to spend
hours walking, talking, and soaking in the sounds and smells of
Argentina.

First Methodist, where E. Stanley Jones had preached every
night for a week in the 1950s, is a national historical site. Its wooden
pews, simple sanctuary, and exemplary pipe organ were built in
1872 and still stand stately amid the skyscrapers of downtown

Buenos Aires. It is often open at noon for prayer, and occasionally the church offers an organ recital at midday as respite for workers on lunch break. The great Argentinian poet Jorge Luis Borges was known to have visited the sanctuary to soak in the ambiance and to remember his great-grandfather, who had been a Methodist preacher in England.[1]

One day Hugo came to the church and entered the side entrance via a long corridor adjacent to the sanctuary. The caretaker of the building met him at the door and said, "There is a priest seated in the sanctuary, waiting for you."

Hugo entered the sanctuary from its rear door, and there he found, sitting contemplatively, the Roman Catholic cardinal of Buenos Aires, Jorge Mario Bergoglio, whom we know today as Pope Francis. They knew each other because both had attended the meetings of the Commission of Christian Churches of Argentina. Hugo greeted the cardinal, who explained that he was just passing by. They sat and chatted about the Week of Prayer for Christian Unity, which the Commission had responsibility for.

They also talked of the ministries that their respective churches held in common. First Methodist Church, along with other Protestant and Roman Catholic churches of the city, worked together in ministries with the homeless and poor. First Methodist's "Solidarity Café" offered hot tea and bread and a place for fellowship and rest each weekday afternoon for people of the street. Other churches offered meals and services in the morning, at noon, or in the evening. It was a short and pleasant visit of one church leader with another.

When Cardinal Jorge Mario Bergoglio was elected pope on March 13, 2013, I exchanged a flurry of e-mails with Hugo. Those of us who lived in the United States were curious about the new pope and eager to hear a word from someone who might know him. Not only did Hugo know the cardinal, now pope, but he was well acquainted with him.

Pope Francis embodies humility in many ways. He eschewed the papal residence, preferring to reside instead in a Vatican guest-house. He dresses in a simpler manner than his predecessors. He has chosen to be transported in a modest Ford Focus while in Rome and a little Fiat motorcar when visiting other countries, rather than in a limousine. He asks people to pray for him. Much has been written about the humility and leadership style of Pope Francis. He had behaved in the same manner while cardinal in Buenos Aires. He preferred taking subways and buses to chauf-feured cars. He lived in a simple, one-bedroom apartment instead of the cardinal's residence.

LESSONS FROM POPE FRANCIS

William Vanderbloemen is a Presbyterian minister and CEO of a company that helps churches with staffing issues.[2] Writing for the online magazine *Fast Company*, Vanderbloemen has identified five lessons that church leaders could learn from the example of Pope Francis.[3]

- *Be accessible.* On his very first day as pope, instead of bless-ing the people, the pope asked the people to bless and pray for him. He writes handwritten thank-you notes. He makes a point of having lunch with the homeless. The les-son: rethink what your most important responsibilities are, keeping in mind that "accessibility sows trust and loy-alty among colleagues."[4]
- *Don't ignore social media.* The pope tweets in eight differ-ent languages and has more than seven million followers

in English. According to Vanderbloemen, communicating via Twitter, Facebook, Instagram, or other social platforms is an effective medium for reaching younger generations. The pope does not pontificate in his tweets. "The Pope's tweets are popular not just because he's the Pope, but because they're humble, inviting, and pluralistic."[5]

- *Flatten your organization.* The pope made choices at the beginning of his papacy that changed the structure of the church. He insisted on being called "Bishop of Rome," rather than "Supreme Pontiff." According to Vanderbloemen, "He took a radical approach to age-old customs and rearranged his management team, reducing its sense of hierarchy," and flattened the organization, allowing him to drive the vision of the church.[6]

- *Take risks.* Early on in his papacy, Pope Francis took risks by reaching out to atheists and agnostics. He softened condemning language toward homosexuals and opened a conversation on forgiveness for women who have had abortions. He did not revise Catholic doctrine; instead, he changed how the church talks about these issues. "His leadership style offered a refreshing new perspective to many who might have previously felt shut out." He took risks.[7]

- *Value input from subordinates.* Pope Francis transformed the Synod of Bishops from a mostly ceremonial group to a decision-making body. He demonstrated through this and public acts how much he values every person. For instance, "he washed the feet of laity prisoners, women, and Muslims, rather than performing the ritual only on priests. He also refocused the role of bishops toward more pastoral activities, premised on the notion that human relationships should be esteemed above all else." The pope's leadership style values what subordinates think and believe. It values the gifts they offer and helps push the organization forward. The pope leads by example and thus cultivates the kind of leadership he values in others.[8]

By choosing the name Francis, after Saint Francis of Assisi, by asking people to pray for him, by many manifestations of simplicity and humility, the new pope, in a short amount of time, has changed perceptions of the Roman Catholic Church. People long for tangible signs that leaders of the church are living examples of the hands and feet of Jesus in the world. Pope Francis has embodied humility. Leaders of new and existing churches are wise to follow his lead and apply these principles to their own context. Be accessible to your community. Show up at town events. Walk the streets. Lead a lean organization.

AMÉRIGO SUÁREZ AND VILLA CONSTITUCIÓN

A much less known but no less valuable servant of God lives 168 miles from Buenos Aires in a little city near Rosario. His name is Amérigo Suárez. In 2010, the Methodist Church of Argentina invited me to give workshops on renewing the church's mission in each of its four regions. In November, I traveled to the Rosario region, where I had served twenty-five years earlier. I rejoiced upon meeting old friends. I got reacquainted with Amérigo Suárez, with whom I had worked when the "Fishers Team" visited his church in Arroyo Seco (see chapter 3).

Amérigo served as a lay leader of his local church. He had visited homes in Arroyo Seco with team members of the Fishers. Soft-spoken and friendly, Amérigo exuded strength as one who knew who he was and to whom he belonged. He knew that Christ had died for him and arose for him and would come again for him.

He was a follower of Jesus. Jesus had entered his life as a young man, and it changed him from a troubled, angry person who drank too much to one who became a good husband and father and who led his local church with grace and understanding.

When I had lived in the greater Rosario area, I visited a church not far from Arroyo Seco, Villa Constitución. It had a reputation for being an inhospitable church. Members fought with members. It was an inward-focused church that had lost its missional connection to the local community. I was not surprised to learn, upon my return to Rosario in 2010, that the church had closed. The building remained, but the congregation had disbanded. Not all churches that close or disband do so because members lack hospitality. Many closed churches were filled with faithful followers of Jesus who lacked the ability or leadership to reach out to their neighbors. Or they were unable to adjust to changing demographics. In the case of Villa Constitución, however, the congregation's demise could be traced to members' behavior.

Then I learned—not from Amérigo himself, but from his area's superintendent—how redemption came for the Methodist witness in Villa Constitución. The closing of the church saddened Amérigo. He lived out a missionary mindset when he saw a need and did something about it. Several times a week for more than a year, he traveled the fourteen miles to Villa Constitución and fasted and prayed in the church's empty worship center. After prayer, he visited homes in the immediate neighborhood.

"I am from the Methodist Church in Arroyo Seco," he would say to whoever answered the door. "I am here to ask for forgiveness for this closed church. Please pray for us and forgive us."

Through his conversations with neighbors, Amérigo found out that the caretaker, who lived in the adjacent parsonage, had a reputation for selling drugs and had been involved in other nefarious activities, including thievery. Amérigo learned that the reputation of the closed church had been further compromised. In addition to the lack of hospitality of the disbanded congregation, there was also someone doing illegal activity on church premises. Though there had never been any arrests, neighbors knew that the caretaker had used the parsonage as a venue to sell drugs. Amérigo spoke to the superintendent, and arrangements were made to replace the caretaker. Amérigo was motivated to continue his practice of prayer and fasting and visiting the neighborhood. In subsequent visits to homes, he asked for forgiveness not only for the closed congregation, but also for what the caretaker had done at the parsonage.

Amérigo listened as neighbors told stories of what had been going on in the mostly vacant premises of the church. Amérigo would nod and say nothing. He wasn't there to defend anyone. He knew the stories to be true. He sought forgiveness, pure and simple. Before leaving the house, he asked people to pray for him.

Neighbors began to recognize Amérigo coming into the area. They would greet him and wave, and some of the homes where he had already visited would invite him in to drink a maté and talk. After a year of prayer, fasting, and visits, a neighbor of the closed church surprised Amérigo.

"We want to pray *with* you," he said. "Would you come by our house next week, so we could pray together? We will invite our neighbors."

Amérigo agreed. The next week he went to the home where he was invited. The host family asked Amérigo to read scripture. They all shared their thoughts and prayed for one another, their neighborhood, Amérigo, Amérigo's church in Arroyo Seco, and the one that had closed in Villa Constitución.

Amérigo continued to travel to Villa Constitución. He formed a prayer group with the neighbors he visited. These people, who heretofore had not attended any church, began to identify these gatherings as *their* church.

Eventually the old church building that had closed was reopened to this emerging community of faith. Amérigo's superintendent not only gave him the keys to the building, but also appointed him as lay pastor of the new community of faith in Villa Constitución. Within a year, fifty people were worshipping in the church.

Then the question, "What can we do to help our neighbors?" became a subject of discussion in the church. "How can we serve our barrio?"

They identified a section of town near the railroad station that had become a shantytown. They began offering food and activities for children and soon formed a branch community of faith among its residents. Now, in addition to those who worshipped in the reopened church building, another twenty to thirty people met for prayer and fellowship at the railway shantytown.

It was authentic humility on the part of Amérigo that began this story of redemption. God was able to use his humility to open doors and to build new relationships and even a new community of faith. The closure of the old church of Villa Constitución was transformed through the humble act of asking forgiveness.

Amérigo and Pope Francis shared a common approach: "Please pray for me." That was the approach that Harry Denman, a lay evangelist in the Methodist Church of the United States, used. E. Stanley Jones also used that approach in India with the creation of a Christian retreat center for prayer.

Jones never sought to belittle or tear down another's belief system. He sought open and honest dialogue. It was a humble approach, but it was not humility based on passiveness. There was nothing wimpy about Jones's invitation to talk about faith. Rather, his humility was born out of the strength of his faith in Jesus Christ. Amérigo's humility was born of a similar strength grounded in faith. Pope Francis, on a much grander stage, offers another example of humility.

These three servants of God demonstrate genuine humility with an overriding interest in the well-being of others. Amérigo had traveled to neighboring Villa Constitución not to start a new community of faith. He went because of a sense of loss and shame that this church, which was part of his family of churches, had misrepresented the gospel of Jesus Christ. It pained him that the congregation's testimony in the barrio was so poor. Amérigo and Jones and the pope were honest about their situations. Amérigo needed to ask for forgiveness for the poor witness of his sister church. E. Stanley Jones had the humility to invite people of other faith traditions into dialogue to discuss the truth of their faith. Pope Francis simply requested, "Pray for me."

ASPIRING TO HUMILITY

"Humility" is a quality of one's character. It shows itself in one's attitude, behavior, and spirit. It respects the other. It so values the other that one is unafraid to ask for forgiveness or to right a wrong. It is the opposite of arrogance, which is based on one's own sense of importance. Arrogance is overbearing and devalues others. Christians become arrogant when they belittle other religions or faith perspectives and when they do not make an attempt to know the people with whom they are relating. The apostle Paul described humility to the church in Philippi when he wrote: "Do nothing from selfish ambition or conceit, but in humility regard others as better than yourselves. Let each of you look not to your own interests, but to the interests of others" (Phil. 2:3-4).

Such humility exalts others. It makes them feel important and valued, and it is a vital part of the missionary mindset. When we carry in our minds that our mission is to lift up the people in this neighborhood, in this town, we open connections whereby the Holy Spirit can begin the work of transformation. Paul said,

"Be transformed by the renewing of your minds, so that you may discern what is the will of God—what is good and acceptable and perfect" (Rom. 12:2). Church leaders who seek to reach their communities with the good news of Jesus Christ need to cultivate humility so they can serve as instruments of God to lift up the spirits of the people.

Stephen Cherry, dean of King's College in Cambridge, England, and an Anglican priest, is the author of several books, including *Barefoot Disciple*, which unpacks what it means to embrace humility today. Cherry talks about humility as the behaviors, attitudes, values, and practices we incorporate into our being that lead us to live more like Jesus. Humble followers of Jesus make God real to others.[9]

Of course, the irony of "humility" is that once you claim to have it, you don't have it. It is a most difficult subject to write or talk about. Cherry contends, "We cannot make ourselves humble. . . . We should *aspire* to humility."[10] It seldom comes to those who seek it. Rather, it flows from one's character.

Church leaders who have a missionary mindset and want to reach their communities for Christ give honor to the gospel when they *aspire* to humility. Such aspiration follows the example of Jesus. It was manifest in the grace that Jesus showed the Samaritan woman at the well and in the examples of Pope Francis, Amérigo, and E. Stanley Jones. We live in the age of the "selfie," when so much attention is directed to ourselves. Moreover, our culture broadcasts the braggadocio of celebrities and politicians as if *that* were something to aspire to.

Aspiring to humility presents an alternative character trait to our current culture, one that draws attention away from ourselves and toward others. When we follow the example that Paul gave to the Philippians, we too put aside our self-interest. We focus on the needs of the larger community.

We can learn three lessons from Paul's letter as we seek to reach people in our community with the gospel of Jesus Christ.

1. DON'T ABUSE POSITION OR POWER

Paul encouraged the Philippians to take on the mind of Christ, who refused to exploit his relationship to God (Phil. 2:5-6). As the text says, Jesus "did not regard equality with God as something to be exploited" (v. 6). When Jesus was challenged by Satan in the wilderness (see Matthew 4:1-11) he refused to yield to the temptations to abuse power (by turning stones into bread), perform spectacular acts (by commanding angels to save him), or claim world dominion (by ruling the kingdoms of the world). There are still towns and cities in the United States that give privileged position to churches. Churches are still exempt (as of this writing) from paying taxes on their property and facilities. A church that wants to avoid exploiting such a privilege might make a donation to the municipality to support services such as fire and police protection. In many communities, clergy are still afforded an exalted status—receiving free membership to clubs or gyms, free entrance to a Friday night high school football game, or a free meal at a meeting of a political party. You can be part of such organizations and go to such gatherings, but offer to pay your own way. Eschew the privilege; show that you are like everyone else and a full participant in community life. Paul's lesson reminds us not to take advantage of privilege but instead to aspire to humility. Paul wrote that Jesus humbled himself by taking the form of a human. Jesus taught as much in the beatitudes (see Matt. 5:3-12). The blessed ones are the ones who seek not the rewards of this world, but the rewards that God gives.

2. BECOME OBEDIENT TO GOD

The second aspect of humility that we learn from Paul deals with obedience. Obedience fosters humility and moves us away from tendencies toward arrogance. When we refrain from supplying all of life's answers from our own perspective and when we put our trust in God, we both adopt and encourage a mindset of humility. We allow Christ to live in us, and we begin to live "by faith in the son of God" (Gal. 2:20). This faith, this trust, becomes possible by humbling ourselves in the way of Jesus. We begin to live out the spirit and invitation of the popular nineteenth-century hymn, to "trust and obey" God.[11]

Jesus showed us obedience in the Garden of Gethsemane. Knowing the imminent danger he faced, he asked God, "Remove this cup from me." Then he showed humility by saying, "Yet, not my will but yours be done" (Luke 22:42). This is obedience that surrenders self to God. E. Stanley Jones understood obedience in this way. Obedience surrenders selfishness, so we can get ourselves out of the way and yield to God's way.

Obedience, for Jones, starts and ends with self-surrender. We set our minds and hearts on following God's way forward. Jones believed that we humans live between the animal kingdom below us and the kingdom of God above us. Through self-surrender, we seek to move toward the kingdom above. We leave behind tendencies of our animal nature, such as selfishness, reliance on brute force, bullying, and manipulating relationships. Instead, we seek the higher ground that desires the well-being of others. With apologies to Paul Anka (and Frank Sinatra), instead of singing "My Way," we sing "God's Way." By surrendering self and striving for obedience to God, we aspire to humility and focus our attention on others.

3. WAIT FOR GOD TO GIVE THE PRAISE

In addition to avoiding abuse of position or power and becoming obedient to God, a third lesson we can learn from Paul is to wait for God to give the praise. When I met with Amérigo Suarez in 2010, after hearing his superintendent's testimony about what Amérigo had done in Villa Constitución, I basked in the presence of a self-surrendered Christian and asked him about his ministry as a lay pastor.

"God is doing wonderful things in Villa Constitución," he said. "New people are coming to faith in Jesus."

Amérigo was humble to the core and gives us an example of someone who seeks God's direction, God's way. As the Bible instructs, if we have been raised with Christ, "seek the things that are above, where Christ is" (Col. 3:1). Amérigo's humility manifested itself in the simple asking of forgiveness. We, too, can visit neighborhoods where churches have closed. We, too, can call on neighbors to ask for forgiveness when the church has failed in its witness.

Paul wrote to the Philippians that God gave Jesus "the name that is above every name" (Phil. 2:9). Jesus never exalted himself. God gave him the glory through the victory of the cross. Jesus was obedient. Jesus surrendered to the cross. God gave him glory so that "every tongue should confess that Jesus Christ is Lord" (v. 11).

When we aspire to humility and we surrender ourselves in obedience to God, we never need to boast of our doings. God will give us the praise if any praise is due. Amérigo has lived that way. He would never characterize himself as being humble. He just is. And because he visited the neighborhood of a closed church with a simple plea for forgiveness and prayer, he opened the hearts of new people who found a new place to gather in fellowship with one another and to be the church that God intended. There is so much we can learn from humble servants like Amérigo, Pope Francis, and E. Stanley Jones. As leaders of new and existing churches, let us remember key practices of a missionary mindset as we aspire to humility and become the hands and feet of Jesus in our neighborhoods:

- Show up: be accessible to the community you seek to reach. Walk the streets.
- Communicate for today's world: use social media.
- Simplify your organization, as Pope Francis did, so newcomers have easy access to your ministry.
- Take risks: show that you love and care about *all* your neighbors.
- Value input from your team. Listen to them and incorporate their ideas.
- Don't brag about yourself. Aspire to humility. Let God receive the praise.
- Don't belittle other people's religion or opinions. Respectfully disagree without disrespecting the other.
- Trust God and obey. It's the better way.

YOUR TURN:
QUESTIONS FOR REFLECTION AND DISCUSSION

1. What lessons do you take from the example of Pope Francis?

2. Have any churches in your area closed or been disbanded? Do you know the reasons? Is there anything you and the congregation you serve can do in the wake of the closure?

3. What does the story of Amérigo teach you about humility? How can his story help you aspire to humility?

4. How can we help one another to humble ourselves, be obedient to God, and to wait upon God for any praise?

6

LOVE

MAKING IT REAL

Emphasize love and make it your working force, for love is central in Christianity.

—MAHATMA GANDHI[1]

The story of Facundo could be the story of just about any church—that is, any church that ever put on a children's Christmas pageant. Please indulge me as I paint a picture of a particular pageant—based on a true story—of a church I served in Rosario, Argentina.

Peace Community Church was an intimate community of faith. Their worship center, converted from a neighborhood house, had been built to accommodate up to sixty people. Relationships among members felt like family. They were never insular, however. The church carried from its earliest days a keen sense of mission. They had run their own nursery school out of church facilities for years, serving the immediate neighborhood with quality child care for preschool children at an affordable cost.

This little congregation of some fifty people took on the responsibility for managing a school for mentally and physically challenged children. The school was located within ten blocks of the church and had been foundering. In a partnership with the municipality, church members began pulling together resources from the community and beyond to make the school a better place to serve the children. In their predominantly Roman Catholic context, the little church was loved by its neighbors and carried a reputation as a caring community of faith. They carried out ministry that was fun and good.

One Christmas week, on a Saturday evening, Peace Community had gained permission from the local police to close off the street so they could put on a Christmas pageant for the neighborhood. They took chairs from the worship center and placed them in the street, facing the church building. The youth and children of the church—dressed as shepherds or wise men or the innkeeper and, of course, as Mary and Joseph—reenacted the events of Jesus' birth. (The babe was a doll dressed in swaddling clothes.) Late December is summer in the southern hemisphere, and temperatures were warm. It was a very pleasant evening.

Church members placed a loudspeaker on the roof, so people could hear recorded music and the dialogue of the children. Filling the seats were neighbors from a three-block radius: Roman Catholics, Protestants, Pentecostals, and those who professed no religion at all. They procured a real donkey to transport "Mary" past the front of the church. The church's front door served as the inn. They had rehearsed a number of times without the real donkey. The children knew their parts. The neighbors were there in full force. All was seemingly ready.

The role of the innkeeper went to Facundo, a twelve-year-old boy who had already grown to six feet tall. Facundo was the church caretaker's son and lived in the rear of the property. While large for his age, he was gentle of spirit. All the children loved him. He was at every activity the church undertook. With the music playing softly from the roof, Joseph led the donkey that carried Mary and stopped in front of the "inn" and knocked.

Facundo opened the door and stood in the doorway. When he saw the donkey and Mary sitting on it, his eyes grew wide. He had been given two lines, the first of which was: "There is no room in the inn." Later he was to say, "We have a stable you can use."

"Joseph" asked for a room, which was the cue for Facundo's first line. Facundo kept looking at Mary on the donkey and said nothing. One could hear soft, nervous laughter coming from the audience. A prompter from behind the church door softly repeated Facundo's line. Finally, after what seemed like an eternity, Facundo said his line aloud.

Joseph insisted. "But we have come from a long journey, and my wife is due to have a baby."

Facundo looked at the donkey that carried Mary and looked at Mary. The prompter whispered his line once again from the other side of the door.

"There is no room in the inn," repeated Facundo, this time with hesitancy. He stood in the doorway, watching.

Joseph insisted again. "We are so tired; do you know anywhere we can stay?"

This was the cue for Facundo's second line. He looked at the donkey and Mary and Joseph. The prompter softly said his line from the other side of the door.

Again, a nervous murmur came over the audience. The prompter repeated the line.

Facundo stood still, looking at the couple. Then he blurted out, "You can have my room!" pointing to the rear of the church property.

There was silence.

Joseph just looked at Facundo and said nothing. It wasn't supposed to have played out in this way. If Facundo had said his lines correctly, Mary and Joseph and the babe would have gone to the end of the sidewalk in front of the church, where there was a "stable" prepared for them.

Finally, Mary broke the ice.

"Okay," she said. "That's really nice of you." She dismounted from the donkey.

The caretaker led the donkey away, and Joseph and Mary went through the door to the "inn" to stay in Facundo's room.

The audience burst into applause. The children took their bows. The pageant could not have been scripted any better. Facundo stole the show and the hearts of the neighborhood. He had captured the meaning of Christmas, because he had made room for the Christ child in his life. It was the most wonderful Christmas pageant ever.

Facundo showed us a way to love.

UNCONDITIONAL LOVE

Love lives at the heart of the gospel of Jesus Christ. As church leaders seeking to reach our communities with that gospel, all of our endeavors, all of our actions, all of our outreach should flow out of the agape love that Jesus embodied in his earthly ministry. *Agape* is the Greek word for unconditional love. It goes deeper than *philia* (brotherly) love and is different from *eros* (romantic) love. Jesus gave the command to "love one another. Just as I have loved you, you also should love one another. By this everyone will know that you are my disciples, if you have love for one another" (John 13:34-35). Paul wrote to the Corinthians that "love is patient; love is kind" (1 Cor. 13:4). Both Jesus and Paul use the term *agape*—love that is self-giving and unselfish, that expects nothing in return.

When we hear stories of how people selflessly sacrifice for the sake of others, we gain a glimpse of humankind's possibility. More often than not, such sacrifice involves the kind of self-awareness we have mentioned and the ability to separate oneself from default cultural understandings. When Jackie Robinson broke the color line in Major League Baseball in 1947, he refrained from his natural (default) tendency to strike back at those who taunted and insulted him for his race. Robinson was a Christian and a Methodist (as was Branch Rickey, who signed him), and I imagine that he knew that such restraint was for a greater good: love. He understood that he had to show by example that nonviolent response to verbal and physical violence would win people's hearts not only for himself, but for all people of color who would come afterward to play professional baseball or work in an office or teach at a school.

Jackie Robinson was still playing baseball when I was in early childhood. I grew up in a mostly white neighborhood, and Jackie's name bespoke respect, excellence, class, and champion. His actions on the field of play won the hearts of people—black and white—and did more than anything else I can remember to help change race relations.

Love that plays itself out in selfless, agape actions holds the promise of inspiring people to be better than they otherwise would be. Unfortunately, the reverse is true as well. When people purport to be Christian but their actions betray the example of Jesus, the witness of Christianity and the church suffers great damage.

E. Stanley Jones referred to ways the Christian church damages its name by not living up to the way of love exemplified in the life of Jesus. In his first book, *The Christ of the Indian Road*, he called this failure to love "the Great Hindrance."

E. STANLEY JONES AND THE GREAT HINDRANCE

The Christian witness is hindered when Christians fail to love. For E. Stanley Jones, writing in 1925, that lack of love was manifest through racism, accepting war as an answer to conflict, and unfair immigration legislation. It is sad that these issues are as germane today as they were many years ago. Jones might observe that the issues are still real because we Christians fail to love the way Jesus taught us to love. Jones constantly challenged Christians to live in a way that was congruent with their professed faith and matched by actions.

These three issues are not the only obstacles that hinder the witness of the church in our age. We will discuss other issues that Jones addressed in chapter 8 when we enter more fully into Jones's understanding of the kingdom of God. However, the three hindrances—racism, war, and unfair immigration practices—speak of missed opportunities to manifest agape in our time and thus reach our communities with the truth and practicality of the gospel.

Jones wrote of the "snobbery" exhibited when white men from the West behaved as if they were superior to people of color in India and South Africa. He also addressed the unchristian behaviors of U.S. citizens with regard to race relations. Jones wrote that the Indian Asians, as subjects of a British colony, knew enough about Christianity as a religion that they were able to identify incongruences in its practice. The Indian Asians knew that racist attitudes tear down everything Christians attempt to teach. Moreover, the Indian Asian, from the knowledge his people had gained about Christ, "knows that these things are not Christian."[2]

Jones recounted how Mahatma Gandhi, when living in South Africa, was refused admission into a Christian church because of his race. Gandhi commented that Jesus himself would have been turned away from the church because he, too, was a person of color. Indian Asians, he said, had every right to judge Christians for these manifestations of unloving behaviors.

Jones recounted how a Hindu person he knew made the distinction between calling someone a Christian man or woman—where "Christian" is an adjective—and calling a person a Christian. The former is a high compliment. A *Christian man or woman* is held in high esteem because others see the spirit of Jesus in that person. However, in India during Jones's day, calling a person a *Christian* connoted that the person was part of an institution that practiced racism, a civilization (i.e., the United States) where people who professed to be Christian lynched black people, and a country that professed faith in the Prince of Peace but for whom war was often the answer to conflict. The incongruities between the agape embodied by Jesus and the behaviors of Christians were a great hindrance to the acceptance of the gospel.

Many people who live in our towns and cities and who are sought after by new church planters carry the same skepticism Hindus did in Jones's day about the inconsistency between what Christians profess to believe and the way they behave. They want to know: Do these people exemplify the spirit of Jesus? Do they embody the values of agape, which accepts them where they are and who they are? Or do they more readily reflect a larger culture that *says* it is Christian but perpetuates the sin of racism, that champions war more than peace, and that is inhospitable to the immigrant?

About the time that Jones wrote *The Christ of the Indian Road*, the United States government passed the Johnson-Reed Act, an immigration law limiting the number of immigrants to the country by strict quotas based on the percentage of a given nationality already living in the United States at the time of the 1890 census. It completely barred immigration from Asian countries.[3] Jones decried the law as racist. "Do not misunderstand me," wrote Jones. "I am not advocating the flooding of America by immigrants."

But Jones advocated that the standards for entry into the United States be applied to nations alike "regardless of their race, color, or nationality."[4]

We are still embroiled in vehement arguments about how we treat immigrants in the United States. As we seek to reach new communities that are composed of people who come from different countries, will our behaviors demonstrate an ethic of agape love, that sees and accepts them unconditionally, or will our actions expose xenophobia? Like Jones, almost a century ago, I do not advocate unremitting immigration. I do believe that our actions and our policies should include rational conversation that addresses all of the complexities of the issue and involves the voices of immigrants themselves.

Regardless of the issue at hand, the missionary mindset begins with love—love of a people you do not yet know. We look for the Christ in them. We live out our faith in a way that opens the possibility that the Christ in us meets the Christ in them. To do so we need to exhibit the meaning of "a Christian" that a Hindu girl gave to E. Stanley Jones: "One who is different from all others."[5]

The difference is marked by love. The Christian wants the best for the people encountered. The Christian wants justice, fairness, and equal opportunity. When the Christian leader enters into a new missionary area, he or she needs to discover the circumstances of life that hinder justice and fairness and to work with people and the powers of that area to redress circumstances that hold people down.

Gandhi's Advice to Christians

When E. Stanley Jones asked Mahatma Gandhi for advice, he identified the great hindrances to Christianity's being accepted in India. Jones had asked Gandhi how Christians could make Christianity something natural in India, something that was not foreign. Gandhi articulated four ways Christianity could be accepted as normal in India.[6]

1. ALL OF YOU CHRISTIANS, MISSIONARIES AND ALL, MUST BEGIN TO LIVE MORE LIKE JESUS CHRIST

It is more important today to imitate Jesus rather than worship him. Don't get me wrong. I believe it is very important to come together to worship God. The circumstances of our day, however, call us to imitate Christ even more than worship him. People want to see the Christian way lived out in daily behavior, as Pope Francis has done so effectively by eschewing the trappings of wealth that come with the office of pope. People want to see congruence between what we believe and how we behave. Gandhi knew this to be true. He wanted to see followers of Jesus act more like Jesus. If we were to approach others in this way, we would be irresistible. People would be drawn to our aspirations to humility. They would be attracted to the way we respect cultures different from our own and would want to join us as we selflessly ministered to others in need. This is a great challenge to church leaders who seek to reach their communities with the gospel, because it means that we must strive to imitate Jesus in the day-to-day actions of our lives. That's hard! We are only ordinary humans. While we know that the challenge is great, we can endeavor to live out a "missionary mindset" that imitates Jesus when we interact with people.

First United Methodist Church of Pahokee, Florida, illustrates how the love of God can help bring healing and hope to one of the most rejected groups of people in our society. This church is living out a missionary mindset with residents of a nearby apartment complex that houses hundreds of former sex offenders.

Sometimes referred to as a modern-day "leper colony," the Pelican Lake apartments was built as duplex housing for migrant workers. While migrant workers still occupy some of the residences, today the apartments mostly house former sex offenders who have finished serving time in prison and are now attempting to reintroduce themselves into society. First United Methodist has accepted residents of Pelican Lake, now known as Miracle Village, into their church community. Some are in leadership roles and some have become part of the staff. First Coast News, a local television news service in Jacksonville, Florida, reported on the unique ministry of First United Methodist and the former sex offenders.[7]

It did not happen without great consternation on the part of church members. The Reverend Patti Aupperlee, pastor of First United Methodist, said that one member, Lynda Moss, angrily confronted her about the idea of inviting residents of Miracle Village to church. "Those people can't come here," said Moss. Others in the congregation worried for the safety of their children. When they began to get to know the residents—all nonviolent sex offenders—church members' attitudes began to change. They began to see them as human beings, and to listen to their stories and their confessions. Some of the residents joined the choir, and others have become leaders. Lynda Moss said that the presence of the former sex offenders in her church caused her to reflect deeply on her faith. "What are we called to do as Christians? What are we called to do? If I don't love a sex offender," she added, "then I'm not loving Christ." She now says that the ministry to Pelican Lake residents reflects a fundamental Christian value.[8]

Reverend Aupperlee herself was a victim of a sex crime when she was a child. She was molested by a friend of her parents. "And I never told a soul—because it must've been my fault." The man was never caught, she reported. Reverend Aupperlee does not see any purpose in demonizing residents of Pelican Lake. "The folks that are here in the village, they're in counseling, they've gone to jail, they've faced their accusers. They've been humiliated, mortified—and they're repentant," said Aupperlee.[9] She said that former sex offenders have difficulty moving on in life after prison. Yet God created us all in his image. God's grace should be available to all. She envisions a church that provides a space where offenders can take advantage of a safe support system as they find health, accountability, and healing. She also believes that victims need a safe place to talk about what happened to them in order to find healing. Living with the pain of sexual unhealthiness is dangerous when lived in isolation.

> But the Pharisees and their teachers of religious law complained bitterly to Jesus' disciples, "Why do you eat and drink with such scum?"
>
> Jesus answered them, "Healthy people don't need a doctor—sick people do. I have come to call not those who think they are righteous, but those who know they are sinners and need to repent." (Luke 5:30-32 NLT)

When we live more like Jesus, we love more unconditionally. We look for the best in others, even those whom our society rejects as living pariahs, and we help others achieve their best. When we carry this love and this imitation of Jesus to our neighbors, others will know who we are by the love we embody. We will get a reputation for treating people fairly.

2. PRACTICE YOUR RELIGION WITHOUT ADULTERATING IT OR TONING IT DOWN

E. Stanley Jones commented on Gandhi's warning against watering down Christianity that instead of presenting our faith boldly and simply and in its rawest form, Christians emasculate it by offering mild forms of Christianity, so as not to offend others. When we do so, we betray the fact that we do not believe Christianity is realistic because it is impossible to truly live like Jesus in the world. Jones wanted India to take up *real* Christianity. Our church leaders today should want the same: to present real Christianity with its radical agape, its message of grace to the downtrodden, the poor, and the marginalized. *Real Christianity*, for Jones, puts into practice the teachings of Jesus in everyday life. It is not something we should shy away from.

John Wesley had a similar focus. He wanted to reintroduce real Christianity into Christendom through Jesus followers who lived out agape in their everyday life. These real Christians, he taught, practice both personal and social holiness by acts of piety and works of mercy. In their personal lives, they read the Bible, pray, fast, worship with others, and study the scriptures (personal holiness). In ministry to others, they visit the sick and imprisoned, relieve the suffering of the hungry and naked, and advocate for the elimination of such social ills as slavery (social holiness). The early Methodists gained a reputation for the love they lived out in everyday life. Methodists were known as people who avoided doing harm to others and looked to do good in every possible situation. You don't have to be an early Methodist to be characterized in this way. A person of any denomination— or any religion, for that matter—can make agape the driving force in life.

As Christian leaders involved in our communities, we will have opportunities to explain how our perspective on a given issue flows from our faith. While we need to be sensitive to other perspectives in a context of religious and philosophical diversity, we should not be afraid to be who we are. Embodying agape will stop us from disrespecting other people's point of view. At the same time, we will stand firm on the foundations of our faith. "I respect your position, even though it is not the same as mine."

3. EMPHASIZE LOVE AND MAKE IT YOUR WORKING FORCE, FOR LOVE IS CENTRAL IN CHRISTIANITY

This third statement of advice by Gandhi is the epigraph for this chapter. Gandhi, a Hindu, knew the power of love as told in the gospel. Jones interpreted Gandhi's statement emphasizing love as pointing to a whole way of life that encompassed the political, the economic, and the religious. He linked Gandhi's comment with *satyagraha*, the nonviolent method of battling conflict in the world that Gandhi used to confront imperialist British rule. Jones believed Christians need to take seriously Jesus as "Prince of Peace" and be formidable proponents of exhausting every method possible to avoid war and violence as a means to resolve conflict. He advanced the idea of taking up Gandhi's nonviolent method to redress racism in the United States.

The key phrase of Gandhi's statement is "for love is central in Christianity." Loving others as a way of being is at the root of the Christian religion. Agape desires the best for humanity—all humanity. It does not countenance circumstances that cut people down and that systematically create situations where people suffer want, hunger, exploitation, disease, and violence. Christian leaders who desire to have an impact on their communities will seek congruence between faith and action that *does no harm*, that *does good*, and that expresses the love of God in the world.

The Ginghamsburg Church in Tipp City, Ohio, under the leadership of Pastor Mike Slaughter, saw human misery in southern Sudan and decided to do something about it. In partnership with the United Methodist Committee on Relief, this church has worked in Darfur and South Sudan to build safe water systems, support schools, and construct sustainable agriculture systems that make it more possible for Sudanese people to stay in their homes. They have served refugees who have been displaced by war and conflict and have helped displaced people return home. E. Stanley Jones would lift up what Ginghamsburg is doing as an expression of the social application of love. Many lives have been transformed by these efforts.

4. STUDY THE RELIGIONS OF OTHER FAITH TRADITIONS MORE SYMPATHETICALLY TO FIND THE GOOD THAT IS WITHIN THEM, IN ORDER TO HAVE A MORE SYMPATHETIC APPROACH TO THE PEOPLE

The fourth word of advice from Gandhi urges us to pay attention to other peoples' religions. The United States and European nations include more and more people within their borders who were born into a religion from another tradition. Gandhi's invitation is all-important today: learn about these religions. Gain an understanding of the other religions, so you can understand better the people who practice them. Don't be ruled by fear of what you do not know. Instead, take up the study of Islam, Hinduism, Buddhism, Judaism, and even the religion of "no religion," of the so-called nones who in surveys identify themselves as adhering to no religion at all.

Jones led by example in this area by inviting people of other faith traditions to the roundtable of conversation to discuss the truth as each person knew it. Living agape in our communities does not have to be complicated. It does not have to be overwhelming. Many Christian witnesses have been able to do this. The example of Amérigo Suarez related in the previous chapter illustrates how a man of humble origin was able to interact with others in a community from a standpoint of simple love. Put together a plan whereby the church you lead shows love to immigrant people.

LESSONS OF LOVE FOR THE MISSIONARY MINDSET

What do new church planters and leaders of existing churches need to know to manifest agape as they reach out to their communities? How can they live into the challenge that Mahatma Gandhi laid down to make agape our working force? Gandhi's challenge and the missionary mindset of E. Stanley Jones provide some lessons.

1. BE AUTHENTIC (PRACTICE LOVE THAT IS REAL)

At the first meeting that E. Stanley Jones had with Mahatma Gandhi, Jones read Gandhi the thirteenth chapter of 1 Corinthians. When he finished reading, there were tears in Gandhi's eyes. "How beautiful, how beautiful," exclaimed Gandhi.[10] Jones chose to read this portion of scripture because it describes love in its entire splendor, naming eighteen attributes of love. It tells us what love does not do and what it does. The first thing it says is that "love is patient." Jones wrote that the Latin root of the word "patience" is *pati*, which means "to suffer." Love can suffer. It "has the capacity to take suffering and sorrow patiently."[11]

Carrying this agape into the community, church leaders identify with and have compassion for the sufferings and sorrow of the community. They exhibit a love that is patient. They learn about the ongoing issues and needs of the community and work with other leaders to address them. They talk with people to find out where the community hurts. This can only happen by walking and talking with people on the streets, in the cafés, at parks. Talk regularly to people who interact with the community, like school principals, police officers, real estate brokers. Ask them to identify needs they have seen.

A cluster of churches in a small city in southern New Jersey formed an outreach team. They spoke to the elementary school principal and learned that a high percentage of students did not have adequate footwear. They organized a campaign to collect new shoes, sneakers, and boots, then brought the footwear to the principal so she could distribute them to students in need. Show some love to the community by addressing real needs.

2. BE INCLUSIVE (PRACTICE LOVE FOR ALL)

Changing demographics mean that new neighbors are moving into most of our communities. Even small cities in the Midwest of the United States have had an influx of immigrants that changes the complexion of the area. In Sioux Falls, South Dakota, you see Somalis and Mexicans shopping in area supermarkets alongside farmers whose families were homesteaders more than a century ago. In Edison, New Jersey, you see Indian Asian restaurants and shops in every section of the city. According to a Carsey Institute report on rural America, "The Hispanic population in nonmetropolitan areas grew at the fastest rate of any racial or ethnic group during the 1990s and the post-2000 period."[12] Church leaders who carry unconditional agape into their communities will care about, notice, talk with, and listen to the new neighbors moving into town. They will carry forth a love that is inclusive of all people and will show the love of Christ to people regardless of race, ethnicity, religion, or sexual orientation. See the people in your community as God sees them: a gift of infinite possibility and promise.

3. BE BALANCED (PRACTICE PERSONAL AND SOCIAL HOLINESS)

E. Stanley Jones emphasized the importance of growing in love. "Unless we are growing in love," he wrote in *Victorious Living*, "we are not growing at all."[13] Our example is Jesus. When Jesus knew that his hour had come to depart this world, "having loved his own who were in the world, he loved them to the end" (John 13:1). Jesus loved in life and loved to the very end in death. As followers of Jesus, we, too, are to make love our be-all and end-all. We should practice love in all of our personal and social relationships.

The challenge to church leaders who seek to reach their communities with the gospel of Jesus is to make love central to their mission. A good example can be found in a ministry taking place today in Houston, Texas.

Several years ago I had the opportunity to visit with a young woman who is planting a new community of faith at the Fondren Avenue Apartments, a complex in Houston, Texas, that houses political and economic refugees from around the world. The young pastor, Hannah Terry, is a graduate of the Missional Wisdom Academy, led by Dr. Elaine Heath and Larry Duggins.[14] Reverend Terry lives in intentional community with others in an apartment in the midst of the refugee community. The intentional community that they formed together live by a "rule of life" similar to monastic communities that have formed since the early centuries of Christianity. They have formed a partnership with the Westbury United Methodist Church of Houston. Westbury serves as an "anchor" church for Reverend Terry's intentional community.

Along with Reverend Terry, I visited a family who escaped danger in the Congo, fleeing to Rwanda. They had been in Houston for only four months when we visited them. Reverend Terry, along with others from her intentional community and members of Westbury United Methodist, gather with refugees on Wednesday night for prayer, song, teaching, and fellowship. We met Mukunzi, the father of the family; his wife, Feza; and their children, Jeanne, Kampili, Samuel, and Olivia. This family had been farming for more than twenty years in the Congo. Political conflict forced them to flee their land and seek help in neighboring Rwanda. They spent some time in a refugee camp there. An agency in Houston called Alliance for Multicultural Affairs worked to get this family from the refugee camp to Houston and the apartment complex.

Reverend Terry serves as a human advocate for this African family and others like them, including immigrants from Central and South America, helping them navigate life in the United States and helping them find needed resources and learn useful skills. This ministry is an example of the social application of agape. In their own practice of a "rule of life," Hannah and her intentional community live out personal holiness through prayer, reading of the scripture, and fasting. In their ministry to refugees, they live out social holiness by attending to real-life needs of the new neighbors who have migrated from thousands of miles away.

YOUR TURN:
QUESTIONS FOR REFLECTION AND DISCUSSION

1. What does it mean to "make room" for Jesus today?

2. Where have you seen agape love practiced?

3. What "Great Hindrance" challenges the church today?

4. How can we respond to Gandhi's challenge to Christians to
   a. live more like Jesus?
   b. practice real Christianity?
   c. make love our working force?
   d. learn about differing religious and nonreligious beliefs of the people who live in your area?

7

PLANTING LIKE PAUL
LEARNING FROM ROLAND ALLEN

St. Paul does not repeatedly exhort his churches to
subscribe money for the propagation of the Faith, he is
far more concerned to explain to them what the Faith
is, and how they ought to practice it and to keep it.[1]

—ROLAND ALLEN

We turn to another voice from the past to gain insights on how a missionary mindset could advance and improve the way we go about church planting. A near contemporary of E. Stanley Jones, Roland Allen served as a missionary in North China from 1895 to 1903. He returned from China to serve as a parish rector in the Church of England for several years before focusing his ministry on writing about missionary principles. Two books have received attention over the years: *Missionary Methods: St. Paul's or Ours?* first published in 1912, and *The Spontaneous Expansion of the Church and the Causes Which Hinder It,* first published in 1927.

I became familiar with the latter book while I was serving in Argentina. It had been translated into Spanish in 1970 by Adam Sosa and was still reverberating in church circles when I arrived later that decade. The translation had been published by Methopress, the publishing company operated by the Argentine Methodist Church. Hugo Urcola, my supervisor, extolled Allen's clear picture of how the early church grew. Allen focused on the missionary methodologies of the apostle Paul and made a case that our modern missionary endeavors should follow more closely what the early church did than what our denominational leaders tended to do.

Like E. Stanley Jones, Allen was prescient. He told his son and grandson that his ideas about mission work would not be taken seriously until after his death. He wrote *Missionary Methods* in 1912. It was reprinted in 1927 and then rediscovered in 1962 (fifteen years after his death), when Eerdmans republished it with an introduction by Lesslie Newbigin.[2] It is still in print today. Similarly, *Spontaneous Expansion* was republished in 1962. It is still in print today, published by Wipf and Stock.

Lessons we can learn from Allen are applicable not only for mission work outside of our country, but also for church planting, especially when we consider that our fields of mission in the United States and in other parts of the Western world are increasingly a context of practices from other spiritual traditions. Allen's views on church planting have particular relevance today. Moreover, existing churches can learn from these principles of planting to enhance their own outreach to their communities. New churches, in their efforts to reach new people, often develop strategies that can just as easily be used in existing churches. For instance, new church starts were the first to implement radical forms of hospitality that are used widely in existing churches—practices such as deploying parking lot greeters, setting up "welcome stations," and giving out gift bags to first-time worshippers. In many ways, new church development serves as the "research and development" wing of the church.

Roland Allen was born in England in 1868. He served in Northern China under the auspices of the Society for the Propagation of the Gospel beginning in 1895. The SPG, as the organization was known, had been established in 1701 under the authority of the Anglican bishop of London and by decree of King William III. The original purpose of the society was to spread the ministry of the Anglican church among British colonies. It was under the auspices of the SPG that John and Charles Wesley went to the colony of Georgia to serve as missionaries in 1735. As it evolved over the years, SPG began work in all parts of the world, including not only former British colonies, such as Kenya, but other countries in Africa, as well as India, China, and Japan. In the 1960s SPG merged with several other British mission societies to form the United Society for the Propagation of the Gospel, which is still in existence today.[3]

Allen's missionary service was interrupted in China during the Boxer Rebellion of 1900, when he had to flee the country. He returned to China in 1902 only to stay for a year before ill health forced him to go back to his native England. He served a parish church for a few years and then formed, along with a wealthy Congregationalist layman, Sidney J. W. Clark, and a Scottish Presbyterian missionary physician, Thomas Cochran, an independent missionary research group. Beginning in 1918, Clark became Allen's benefactor, providing him and his family a house and an annual income that allowed him to spend the rest of his working years writing, publishing, and lecturing.[4]

Allen found in Clark and Cochran two people who agreed with his ideas about promoting indigenous church principles. Allen's China experience attempting to proclaim the gospel in a land that was predominantly made up of persons from other faith traditions, and his association with the SPG led him to write critical articles about how mission agencies organized their work. In the 1920s he wrote articles for a quarterly periodical, *World Dominion,* as well as pamphlets such as "Voluntary Clergy" (1923), "Voluntary Clergy Overseas—An Answer to the Fifth World Call" (1928), and "Non-Professional Missionaries" (1929). He urged mission leaders to revisit the methods of the apostle Paul in their organization of mission work.[5]

Newbigin points out in his foreword to the 1962 edition of *Missionary Methods* that the term "methods" is an unfortunate choice of words. Allen insisted that the church should not look for a neat package of principles to follow in its outreach. Rather, we are invited to follow the movement of the Holy Spirit in the work of spreading the gospel of Jesus Christ and planting new churches. Allen believed that mission societies like the SPG did not sufficiently rely on the movement of the Holy Spirit in mission work. Instead of turning over responsibility to indigenous leaders, they relied on efforts by foreign missionaries to control the development of the church. Allen argued that such attempts at control stifled the Spirit's movement and thus served as an obstacle for a more spontaneous expansion of the church led by Christians native to the land.

Allen's reading of the apostle Paul led him to believe that mission-sending societies, or what today we might call denominational staff, perpetuated paternalistic patterns by holding on to control of the mission rather than turning it over to the people with whom they were in mission.

Allen drew from Paul and challenged church leaders to follow four themes:

1. Plant churches that are indigenous.

2. Plant churches that are self-supporting.

3. Train up new followers of Jesus and let them become leaders.

4. Church planters, like the apostle Paul, should work themselves out of a job.

We turn to these principles laid down by Allen as lessons for those who wish to adopt a missionary mindset today.

1. PLANT CHURCHES THAT ARE INDIGENOUS

When I lived in Argentina, I learned a little about wine. Argentina is the fifth-largest producer of wine in the world. I learned the importance of *terroir*, a French term that refers to the character of the land where the grapevines grow. Wine produced in a particular location is influenced by the amount of water available for the vines, the composition of the soil, the amount and angle of sunshine, and how dry or rainy the growing season is. I learned, for instance, that Malbec wine originated in France, where it was used mostly for blending purposes. Grafted vines that were planted in Mendoza, Argentina, produced a much better-tasting wine because of the *terroir* of that area.

When we plant indigenous churches, we show how we value the neighborhood or town we wish to reach. We enjoy the fruit of our listening skills as we connect to the heartfelt needs of the community. We work with people who live in the area because they, more than any outsider, know the personality and culture of the locale. And we just may discover that the *terroir* of this area can produce an altogether more flavorful variety of Christianity.

We have heard from the most successful church planters that their stories of growth were unique to their setting. Rick Warren, who founded the Saddleback Church in 1979, and Adam Hamilton, who founded Church of the Resurrection in 1990, have urged others not to imitate what they did. Rather, they advise, learn the principles that lie behind their success and apply them in your context. This is the process of indigenization.

The root of "indigenous" is the Latin *indigena*, which means "native." Planting churches that are native means that they belong to and originate from a specific locale. What happened at Saddleback is indigenous to Orange County, California. What happened at Church of the Resurrection is indigenous to Leawood, Kansas. What constitutes effective ministry and outreach in Orange County will look different from ministry in Bergen County, New Jersey.

To plant indigenous ministries in a given area, we learn about its customs. Rick Warren surveyed those who were attending worship about the radio stations they listened to, and he used music in his worship services that matched the tastes of the people indigenous to his area.[6] If we were to canvass people for their musical preferences in, say, East Nashville, we would likely discover musical tastes altogether different from those in Warren's community. To make a church plant native to a given locale, we learn the tastes, customs, and preferences of that locale.

In the introduction to this book, we mentioned how Hudson Taylor wore Chinese garb in order to gain a better hearing in China. He captured the significance of indigenization. In preceding chapters, we have encouraged leaders to walk their neighborhoods, talk to people on the streets, in the bars, and in parks. Church leaders do this so they can learn about the needs and concerns, the hopes and possibilities of their locales and ultimately so that they plant indigenous churches.

Judicatories that want to start new churches need to keep this principle of indigenization in mind. As denominational leaders work with existing churches, they should ask themselves how they can best plant churches that truly give expression to the *terroir* of a given area. *Terroir* or indigenization is important because it fits in better with the culture, language, and customs of the area. We want to reach the people living in a given community with language that is understandable to them, music they want to sing, art that inspires them, and a purpose that resonates with the deepest yearnings of their spirits.

2. PLANT CHURCHES THAT ARE SELF-SUPPORTING

The greatest stumbling block to our current church-planting movement is the high cost to denominations. Using a so-called parachute drop strategy, many mainline denominations give new church planters start-up money. Typically, this means that they receive full salary support along with program funds for the first eighteen months, and then the amount of outside funding decreases over the next several years. Under this methodology, a successful church plant should be able to fund its own ministry after three to five years. The overall cost for five years of support can be as high as a half million dollars.

This strategy leads to a successful self-sustaining church less than a quarter to a third of the time, however. Those new church starts that cannot sustain the cost of ministry within the given amount of time are forced to change their course. Some close; others attempt to continue with less than full-time leadership. Church planters feel a great deal of pressure to get their numbers up within their first few years. If they miss the benchmarks established at the beginning of the plant, they feel like a failure.

The high cost has caused some judicatories to abandon plans for new church planting altogether. Judicatory leaders are reluctant to provide denominational funds unless there is sufficient "fruit"—usually measured in average worship attendance—to justify the expenditure. We are discovering that in many parts of the country, particularly the more secularized areas in the northeast and west, this method of creating a self-sustaining church plant is difficult, if not impossible to carry out. Judicatory leadership and church planters will need to think through other ways to plant new churches that are not so dependent on a large outlay of money.

Other church-planting strategies are more cost-effective and have a higher success rate. When an existing church plants a second campus, the success rate is higher than 90 percent. Costs can be shared between the judicatory and the existing church, or in many cases, the multiplying church funds the additional campus by themselves. Yet, even this model is costly when a fully ordained minister is placed and support includes salary, housing, and benefits, even before consideration of the cost of renting and equipping a facility. Existing churches are wary of investing so much money into church planting. Judicatories have limited funding to offer.

Churches that start second campuses are rediscovering the power of deploying laity as church planters. In United Methodist circles, using lay planters is a rediscovery of a method common during the most explosive growth in the denomination's history, the first half of the nineteenth century. Ordained ministers trained up laity to start and lead local congregations. The ordained pastors—called circuit riders—maintained contact with local churches through correspondence and regular visits. From 1800 to 1850, the Methodist movement in the United States grew from several thousand adherents in 1800 to 1.5 million by 1850.

Ken Nash serves as the teaching pastor of Cornerstone Church in the Grand Rapids, Michigan, area. Ken joined the staff of Cornerstone in 2006 and then undertook a study that reexamined the role of laity in church planting. His study became a doctor of ministry dissertation, *The Identifying, Equipping, and Sending of Laypersons to Lead a Multi-site Church*,[7] which was successfully presented to Asbury Theological Seminary in 2014. In it Nash cited studies done at Penn State University that referenced the meteoric rise of early Methodism. Unfortunately, Nash pointed out, citing the research conducted at Penn State University, "the dramatic . . . rise of the Methodists was short-lived. It is instructive to note that the Methodists began to slump at precisely the same time that their amateur clergy were replaced by professionals who claimed episcopal authority over their congregations."[8]

If we were to follow the advice of Roland Allen and the principles of the apostle Paul, we would, as Ken Nash has already done, rely on the gifts and commitment of laity in church planting. Rather than looking to the availability of money to drive the mission, the new church plant would be driven by the Spirit of God and the passionate disposition of baptized Christian laity to reach new people. We would look for ways to fund new churches that deploy bi-vocational and unpaid servants.

As Roland Allen underscored in his books, church planting by the apostle Paul was never contingent on funding. Paul was a bi-vocational church planter, earning his keep as a tentmaker (Acts 18:3). He never spent more than six months in a given church plant. He trained indigenous people, even ordaining them, so they could carry on the work. He maintained contact through correspondence and occasional visits, but left the new church plant in the hands of native people whom he had trained and trusted the Spirit to guide the work.

Allen responded to critics who said that Paul's was a totally different period of time and "that the age of simple expansion has gone by, that we must live in our own age, and that in our age such spontaneous expansion is not to be expected."[9] Allen observed that after many years of missionary activity in Madagascar, the missionaries were driven out of the country. And then, the Christian

church, freed from the control of foreign mission-sending organizations and under persecution in its own country, multiplied
tenfold.[10]

Similar stories have been told of China. Western missionaries left the country and gave up control of the church when the
People's Republic of China was established in 1949. Without outside support or control, a Protestant church was formed, calling itself the Three-Self Patriotic Movement Church. The name
stands for "self-governance, self-support, and self-propagation," a
reminder that all foreign influences had been removed.[11] Yet even
this church was forced to go underground during the Cultural
Revolution of 1966–1976, when religious life in China was essen-
tially banned. When the Three-Self Church reemerged in the late
1970s, the world found out how much Christianity had grown
over the years. Among Protestants alone, adherents to the faith
grew from a million in 1949 to more than 58 million today.[12]

Roland Allen attributed the growth of the church in Madagascar
to the work of the Holy Spirit and the indigenization of the church
and would say the same about China. Churches in Madagascar and
China were let loose of foreign control, and the Spirit worked among
native leadership, so that a "spontaneous expansion" could occur.
The churches in these countries did not receive outside funding
and were not controlled by outside leaders. Yet the Spirit worked
among native Christians to grow the church tenfold and more.

Throughout the apostle Paul's missionary endeavors, according
to Allen, he never sought financial help. While Paul acknowledged
that those who preach the word can rightfully be compensated for
it, he himself did not make claim to such a right (1 Cor. 9:11-12),
because he thought that burdening a congregation with his care
would be a hindrance to the spreading of the gospel of Jesus Christ.
Paul reminded the Thessalonians that he supported himself when
he wrote, "You remember our labor and toil, brothers and sisters;

we worked night and day, so that we might not burden any of you while we proclaimed to you the gospel of God" (1 Thess. 2:9). Paul's financial independence gave him the freedom to preach Christ without any strings attached. And it gave him moral standing among his hearers. "You are witnesses, and God also," he continued, "how pure, upright, and blameless our conduct was toward you believers" (v. 10).

Roland Allen pointed out that the apostle Paul was guided always by the Holy Spirit in his missionary work. It was the Spirit who forbade Paul from speaking the word in Asia (Acts 16:6). When he came to Bithynia, again it was the Spirit who did not allow them to enter the city (v. 7). Paul was led to Macedonia by a vision that the Spirit gave him (v. 9). He worked as a tentmaking, bi-vocational church planter, earning his own keep so that the proclamation of Christ would be received without obstacle—without the interference of money.

Paul took no money from his converts, nor did he take money to them. "There is not a hint from beginning to end of the Acts and Epistles of any one church depending upon another, with the single exception of the collection for the poor saints at Jerusalem," wrote Allen. "That collection . . . had nothing to do with church finance in the ordinary sense. Its importance lay in its demonstration of the unity of the church, and in the influence which such a proof of brotherly charity might have in maintaining the unity of the church."[13] Allen knew that planting churches takes money. He was concerned, however, that an overdue emphasis on raising money can compromise the primary purpose of making disciples. He also was concerned that relying on outside funding to purchase property or facilities creates a burden of dependence on the part of the new church.

The challenge for the church-planting movement in the United States today is to find new ways of funding church plants that are less costly and, as soon as possible, to give control of the mission to those who have their feet on the ground. Judicatories need to find ways to give more freedom to existing churches to plant multiple campuses through the deployment of laity. If we follow the church planting principles of the apostle Paul, we send out bi-vocational church planters as well as trained and committed laity who do not burden new believers with the cost of support.

It's happening. Cornerstone Church in the Grand Rapids, Michigan, area has put into place a methodology for deploying laity in the three new campuses they are starting without reliance on denominational funding. They have a thorough process for identifying new campus pastors, training them and training other laity to support them in the new church plant. The laity who serve as founding pastors of campuses start off as less than full-time workers. They, like the apostle Paul, are bi-vocational. Cornerstone is able to fund additional campuses.

Rosario Picardo is the executive pastor for new church development at Ginghamsburg Church in Ohio. He works with bi-vocational lay pastors as well as volunteer laity to plant new campuses. In the system that Rosario helped create in Ohio, the bi-vocational lay pastors have full-time jobs outside of the church. They plant new churches with the help of laity.

In the metropolitan area of Chicago, Ruben Rivera, a lay church planter, followed the Holy Spirit's lead as opportunities opened up for him to plant a new Hispanic-Latino church. Ruben participated in a two-year academy sponsored by his judicatory to learn about planting new churches. At the conclusion of the training period, a judicatory leader, Martin Lee, challenged Ruben with starting a new church without giving up his day job. Ruben kept his job as a full-time road construction foreman. He gathered around himself other laity, and together they planted a church that within two years had a congregation of 150 people. Rivera's life was turned around by God. "I was addicted to alcohol and drugs for 20 years," said Rivera with tears in his eyes. "One day I prayed to God that he would free me and I promised to serve him for the rest of my life. Today, I am honoring that promise."[14]

Sometimes, we church leaders become paralyzed by the daunting cost of starting new faith communities for new people. We can start small and with little or no funding when we train and empower laity to create new places for new people that expand the reach of the faith to others. It takes courage for judicatory leaders like Martin Lee to identify laity like Ruben Rivera and give them training and then freedom to live out their ministry. It takes vision and bold leadership for bishops, like Deborah Kiesey of Michigan and Gregory Palmer of West Ohio, to support churches like Cornerstone and Ginghamsburg in their efforts to find new ways to reach new people with the gospel of Jesus Christ. These methodologies that deploy gifted laity are much likelier to produce self-sustaining churches, however, than are churches that rely on salary support packages for clergy.

3. TRAIN UP NEW FOLLOWERS OF JESUS AND LET THEM BECOME LEADERS

The strategy employed by the apostle Paul in church planting always included training up new leaders. Wrote Allen: "St. Paul preached in a place for five or six months, and then left behind him a church; not, indeed, free from the need of guidance, but capable of growth and expansion."[15] Allen references Paul's six-month sojourn in Lystra: he ordained elders, left, and did not come back for another eighteen months. He would get the church up and running, leaving behind leaders whom he himself had ordained, and then came back periodically to visit. From the beginning, Paul's strategy was to train up people who could lead the church. But he did not abandon them. He wrote letters addressing specific concerns of specific churches, the letters circulating among a wider audience of churches that wanted to learn as much as possible from Paul. He also sent others from his team (e.g., Barnabas, Apollos, Timothy) to make periodic visits to the churches that had been planted. In this way, local churches became familiar with different leaders.

The United Methodist Church's mission statement is, "Making disciples of Jesus Christ for the transformation of the world." If we take this mission statement to heart, we will look for opportunities at every turn to teach others what we already know. Cornerstone Church in Grand Rapids trains laity in self-awareness, how to deal with conflict, how to mentor other leaders, what it means to follow in the Methodist/Wesleyan heritage, and how to build a team of helpers. The lead pastoral team from the first campus teaches lay church planters how to preach and prepare worship. The Lay Missionary Planting Network curriculum offered by Path 1 also teaches laity the fundamentals of leading a community of faith. When we turn over leadership to laity, the church becomes less dependent on clergy. We also empower laity to take up their own call in ministry.

Judicatory leaders can encourage existing local churches to identify laypeople from their congregations who can take up the challenge to lead new communities of faith. Senior pastors of existing churches should be vigilant in identifying laity who could lead others.

4. CHURCH PLANTERS, LIKE THE APOSTLE PAUL, SHOULD WORK THEMSELVES OUT OF A JOB

The apostle Paul's strategy was always to leave the ministry in the hands of natives. The native church members handled the finances and carried forth the mission. What might this look like in our day? A church planter should carry a missionary mindset that works him or herself out of a job from the outset of ministry. He or she prays that the Holy Spirit brings leaders who can be trained to take on key responsibilities in the church.

When I served in Argentina as a missionary, I was conscious that my tenure would not be long. I tried always to stay in the background of new mission initiatives and give way to leaders—clergy and lay—from Argentina. For instance, when we conducted evangelistic weekends as part of the "Fishers" team, the connectional evangelism program we started in the region of Rosario, I never spoke before a group we were addressing. Team members from the area gave testimony or preached. I reasoned that newcomers coming to church would not want to hear from someone speaking Spanish with a North American accent. Besides, this program had to be indigenous if it was to last.

I didn't really know how long I would be serving in Argentina. Later, when I returned to the United States to serve churches, I never knew how long I would serve in a given pastorate. But I believed that it was important to work myself out of a job. For me, this is a key component of a missionary mindset.

During my first term as a missionary in Dolores, Argentina, I prayed to God for leaders. "Send me someone, O God," I prayed, "who could be a strong example to the people already here of what it means to follow Jesus." God sent not just a person, but two families. I had been serving the church for five months and was leading my first Christmas service. Though the church had a harmonium (a small organ powered by pedals), we had no one to play it. Instead, I accompanied hymns and songs on guitar. As we gathered for the Christmas morning worship service, a young woman came up to me and asked if I would like her mother to play the harmonium. "I would love it!" I responded. Graciela came forward and accompanied all of the traditional Christmas hymns. I met Roberto, her husband. They had been members of a Pentecostal church in town, but their twin daughters had urged them to come to our church. Though he only had a third grade education, Roberto was a gifted preacher. I invited him to preach once a month. I reasoned that at least for one week per month the members of the church could hear a native speaker and not my foreign accent.

In late January, I received a knock on the door from a couple I had never met. They introduced themselves as Gladys and Adamo. They said they just wanted to see the church they would be attending. Adamo had just been transferred as a manager of a major bank for the branch in Dolores. They were Methodist and had been members in a church in another part of the Province of Buenos Aires. Soon I learned that Adamo could preach. Gladys could teach Sunday school. By February I was able to reduce my preaching to once every other week.

The Spirit blessed the church abundantly. I now had more time to prepare what usually ended up being two sermons a month. Adamo was a forceful and dramatic preacher. Roberto's style was more soft and gentle. The three of us made a good team, and before long attendance at the church grew. In fact, it multiplied by a factor of seven! Of course, we began with an average attendance of five, so when we hit thirty-five, we were all very happy! Any credit goes to the Spirit of God, who answered my prayers and sent two families to the church that made all the difference in the world. When I finished my term as pastor, Adamo and Roberto continued to preach alongside the newly appointed pastor, and the church remained strong. I had hit upon a strategy: get out of the way whenever the Spirit showed me a way to do so. Turn ministry over to people indigenous to the area. Give responsibility to those whom the Spirit sends you.

The danger of not working ourselves out of a job is that we make ourselves indispensable. I am not suggesting that we should go back to the days of very short pastorates. There can be huge benefits to long pastorates. Mike Slaughter will have served thirty-eight years as senior pastor of Ginghamsburg when he is scheduled to retire. Because the church has multiplied its ministry through multiple campuses, Mike's legacy should live far into the future. Here it is good to remember Stephen Covey's advice "to begin with the end in mind."[16] How will you hand off your ministry once your tenure finishes? At the very least, if you have been serving in a long pastorate, work with leaders of the church on a transition strategy.

There are all kinds of reasons we do not like to do this. We like to be in a particular role of leadership, and we like to stay there. We enjoy being the center of attention. Or, for laity, we like the influence we can have as chair of the church council or head of the finance committee. When we hold on to leadership positions too long, though, we stifle the possibility of growth on the part of others. Roland Allen wrote that we should never give the impression that the mission depends exclusively on us. We should always look for ways to hand off ministry to others. "Christianity is a principle of life," wrote Allen.[17] It is not meant to be an institution. It is meant to be a movement of the Spirit. When we tend toward institutionalization, we sap the spiritual nature of our work and ministry. We stifle the growth and Christian maturation of others.

I learned this at an early age. In my home church we had a large youth group. Each year in May, before going on summer break, we would elect officers for the following academic year. Several upperclassmen approached me when I was a freshman about taking on the responsibility of being treasurer. They wanted to put my name on the slate of nominations.

"What do I know about being treasurer?" I protested.

"Don't worry," they responded. "We will teach you. We think you have the gifts."

They empowered me and gave me confidence where I thought there to be none.

The high school youth group is by nature a place where people don't stay very long. The youth knew that they had to be on the lookout for new leaders all the time. In a natural way they lived a missionary mindset and worked themselves out of a job. They had to. Adults could learn a lesson. We need to pray to God to give us the eyes to see who among our newcomers can take on new responsibilities. We need to be open to the Spirit of God to help us find and mentor the people who can begin to take on responsibilities.

The key challenge for judicatory leaders and pastors of existing churches is to rediscover the gifts of laity in the planting of new faith communities. We are invited to learn from Roland Allen's study of the apostle Paul that church planting should be driven by the Spirit of God and not be dependent on the availability or lack of funds. Clergy are invited to create systems whereby they train up laity to do the work of planting churches; where the clergy themselves serve as mentors and teachers; and where the entire endeavor of creating new places of faith for new people is infused and led by the Spirit of God.

YOUR TURN:
QUESTIONS FOR REFLECTION AND DISCUSSION

1. Describe a time when the mission of the church has been driven not by the Spirit but by the availability or lack of money.

2. What can our churches do to mitigate the pull of "money and control" and rely more on the Spirit for direction?

3. When have you witnessed a Christian leader working himself or herself out of a job in a positive way?

4. Why is it important that new ministries become self-governing, self-supporting, and self-sustaining?

8

THE KINGDOM

LIVING AND BREATHING
THE GOOD NEWS

*The Kingdom of God . . . meant nothing less than
replacing this present unworkable world order, based
on greed and selfishness, with God's order.*[1]

—E. STANLEY JONES

A missionary mindset presents the gospel of Jesus Christ to people so they have an opportunity to be transformed. We serve as instruments of God's unfolding kingdom to help people come into a real and permanent relationship with God. This relationship brings assurance of everlasting life and incorporates us into God's community, which addresses the systemic evil of tribes and nations and of principalities and powers. A missionary mindset is clear about the essentials of the gospel as we work to reach our communities with good news. As we learn from E. Stanley Jones how to reach our communities, we keep in mind the essential witness to others that "Christ has died, Christ is risen, Christ will come again." These essentials come into focus when we revisit the lessons that Jones taught concerning the kingdom of God. As a young minister serving thousands of miles from home, I became acutely aware of the systemic sin present in human attempts to order life. I also found direction in the writings of E. Stanley Jones on the kingdom of God. Let me explain.

When I arrived in Argentina in the fall of 1978 to serve as a missionary in the Methodist church, a military dictatorship ruled the country. In every direction, as soon as I exited the customs area at Ezeiza airport, I saw machine gun–toting soldiers keeping watch. I would see them on the streets in downtown Buenos Aires. I saw them guarding the then-vacant congress building on my way to Spanish class.

For me to live in a country under military dictatorship was a rude awakening. I did not fully understand the reasons why leaders of the army, navy, and air force thought it necessary to overthrow a democratically elected government, dismiss congress, and put the country into "lockdown" mode. I felt the tension in the air. When I asked a member of the church I was assigned to serve what was behind the military's actions, he said, "The country was in chaos. We needed order restored. The military was the only entity capable of doing that." Most members of the English-speaking church I served on an interim basis—while I studied Spanish— agreed with the military takeover. They had friends who had been kidnapped by leftists and held for ransom, and they believed that the military would put an end to these kidnappings.

I also heard stories from pastors and friends who were members of the Spanish-speaking Argentinian churches. They told me of clandestine prisons that held "disappeared" persons who had been captured in the night by paramilitary squads bent on ridding the country of what the military rulers deemed subversive.

"Paramilitary squads" were small, anonymous groups organized by military leaders but not officially part of the armed forces. Members of these groups included retired military officers, police personnel, and others especially recruited to kidnap people who had some connection to those associated with leftist antigovernment organizations. According to the book *Guerrillas and Generals: The "Dirty War" in Argentina* by Paul H. Lewis, a professor of political science at Tulane University, the active military officers "were unwilling to soil their own hands" by going after those associated with the left-wing organizations.[2]

The official report by the commission that investigated the disappearance of people in Argentina, of which Methodist bishop Carlos Gattinoni was a member, also referred to actions by anonymous groups. A majority (62 percent) of those who were detained and never reappeared were taken from their homes in the middle of the night. Others who became "disappeared" were taken on the streets (24.6 percent), at work (7 percent), or at their place of study (6 percent). Less than one-half of 1 percent of the disappeared were legally detained by the military or the police.[3]

My Argentinian friends told me of church leaders and the sons and daughters of church leaders who were taken and never heard from again. They told me that they had been taken away because of the hint of solidarity with the so-called subversives. It was scary and unlike anything I had experienced in life. A friend who was sympathetic to the military told me that if the government captured one true "leftist" out of a hundred, if was worth the effort.

In the first months of living in a northern suburb of Buenos Aires, as a newcomer to Argentina, I became immersed in a real-life "Political Science 101" course that opened my eyes to realities I had never known. The curriculum was filled with stories of governments that killed its own citizens and reminded me of the horrors of world war, the attempts of one country's government to impose itself on others—stories of death, destruction, broken promises, and hopelessness. The parsonage where we lived was located ten blocks from the home where Adolf Eichmann had been captured. Eichmann, the architect of the Nazi plan to implement the "Final Solution" of eradicating Jews in Europe, had successfully hidden his identity for ten years before being hunted down by Israeli secret service in May 1960. Stories swirled in the neighborhood of other Nazi escapees who had lived nearby.

We also heard stories of Juan Perón; his wife, Eva; and the Argentinian version of national socialism. Some people exalted the Peróns as saviors, while others decried them as having squandered the riches of the country. Juan Perón served as president of Argentina from 1946 until 1955, when a military coup removed him from power and forced him into exile. Perón returned from exile in 1973 to run for the presidency. He was elected at the age of seventy-seven, but served only eight months before he died on July 1, 1974. His third wife, Isabel (Eva was his second wife; his first wife, Aurelia, had died in 1938), who had run as his vice president, became president upon Juan's death. It is beyond the scope of this book to go into the details of this volatile political period in Argentina's history, but it is important to remember that the seeds of the military's abuse of power were sown in the events that led up to the return and reelection of Juan Perón in 1973. This is also the turmoil in which I served the Argentinian Methodist church.

My education was not limited to events in Argentina itself. Our own country, the United States, was vilified by Argentine friends for the debacle of the Vietnam War, which had ended only a few years before we arrived. A Chilean pastor serving in the city of Buenos Aires had escaped the dictatorship of Augusto Pinochet in neighboring Chile, a regime that also imprisoned or put to death people associated with a democratically elected government.

As a young Christian leader who was just starting his career, I wondered if the church could really make a difference in such a world. Can the church transform the human tendency toward violence, greed, and selfishness? How can the church give witness to the love of God in the face of military might that violates the rights of people? How can it instill its values based on the teachings and example of Jesus in a way that could make a real difference and not be relegated to a nebulous spiritual netherworld?

One option for the church is to ignore politics and keep a distance from anything that has to do with current events. Yet, such silence in the face of abuse of power will be viewed by victims of such power as complicity. I was fortunate to witness a church that chose a different option, one that in many ways spoke truth and promoted human dignity to the forces of darkness and death. In the face of atrocious violations of human rights, the Evangelical Argentine Methodist Church and its leaders, putting their own lives at risk, decried the government's participation in the disappearance of people. Bishop Gattinoni and, later, Bishop Pagura, along with many other clergy and laity, exhibited courageous leadership during perilous times. They could have been taken away by paramilitary squads for speaking out against government actions. But for Gattinoni and Pagura, the violation of human rights went against the gospel of Jesus Christ and his teachings, and they could not be silent.

Pagura, who served as bishop during the entire time I lived in Argentina, preached Jesus and cited the gospels in his sermons and speeches. He referred to Jesus' teachings on peacemaking in the Beatitudes (Matt. 5:9) and the judgment of the nations (Matt. 25:31ff). He hammered at the importance of attending to human need. He spoke on Paul's teachings not to repay evil for evil (Rom. 12:17); the grace that Jesus showed tax collectors (Mark 2:15-17) and prostitutes (Matt. 21:30-32); and Jesus' love, grace, and respect for human beings, in contrast to the harsh order imposed by the Roman military government.

Pagura spoke truth to power. In his sermons and his letters to local churches, he reminded us of the words of the book of Hebrews: "Remember those who are in prison, as though you were in prison; those who are being tortured, as though you yourselves were being tortured" (13:3).

Based on these and many other biblical teachings, Pagura and other Argentine Methodist leaders did not hesitate to speak out. They believed that the gospel of Jesus Christ addressed the whole of humanity in all of its personal and social spheres. Theirs was a tiny but potent voice. Despite a membership of only ten thousand, a letter from Bishop Pagura or a resolution from an official gathering of the Evangelical Argentine Methodist Church would be published by the most widely circulated newspapers, such as *El Clarín* in Buenos Aires. In contrast, the Roman Catholic Church, which claimed 80 percent of the country's population and which was composed of fourteen ecclesiastical provinces, was largely silent during the years of military rule, with the exception of two outspoken bishops: Jorge Novak (Quilmes) and Jaime de Nevares (Neuquén). De Nevares, along with Bishop Carlos Gattinoni of the Methodist Church, helped form the Permanent Assembly for Human Rights, which worked tirelessly to redress injustices perpetrated by the government.

The courageous actions of Argentine Methodist leaders drew richly from their Wesleyan heritage. Nellie Ritchie served as bishop of Argentine Methodists from 2001 to 2009. Reflecting on the attitude of the Evangelical Argentine Methodist Church during the years of the military dictatorship, Bishop Ritchie said that "as Methodists we have inherited an ecclesiology that makes us emphasize faithfulness to the Kingdom of God over the church as an institution. If, as John Wesley said, 'the church is an instrument of the Kingdom . . .' then this tool of the kingdom should be placed at the service of those for whom the Lord of the kingdom—Jesus Christ—gave his life."[4]

As inheritors of Wesleyan theology and practice, Argentine Methodists share with Methodists from around the world an emphasis on both personal and social holiness. Wesley believed that spirituality is deeply personal and should be lived out through individual and corporate practices of piety, such as reading the Bible, praying, fasting and worshipping regularly. Wesley also believed that Christians need to attend to social holiness—to work in ministries of mercy that alleviate suffering in society. These, too, have their individual and corporate dimensions: doing good works, visiting the sick, visiting those in prison, feeding the hungry, and giving generously for the needs of others. As a corporate expression of the body of Christ, leaders of communities of faith who have a missionary mindset will also live out both personal and social holiness.[5]

E. STANLEY JONES ON THE KINGDOM OF GOD

Argentina was still ruled by a military dictatorship when I began my second term as a missionary in March 1982. That same month I was given an assignment by my supervisor, Hugo Urcola, to lead an evangelization initiative for the region. I struggled to present the gospel in this context of repression and abuse of power. When in my search for resources I came across the teachings of E. Stanley Jones on the kingdom of God, I discovered writings that made sense to me. I began to see a real connection between Wesley's wisdom about keeping a balance between personal and social holiness and Argentine Methodists' courageous witness during military rule. I was struck by Jones's clear emphasis on the kingdom of God as a way to order life. I developed a hope that the church *could* make a difference in the world if it found a way to live more closely to the values and design of the kingdom of God as taught by Jesus.

What is the kingdom of God? It is a comprehensive new reality where God's rule, grace, justice, and mercy are practiced. Jesus began his ministry by proclaiming it: "The time is fulfilled, and the kingdom of God has come near; repent, and believe in the good news" (Mark 1:15). In the Sermon on the Mount, Jesus invited hearers to "strive for" it and not to worry about everyday needs, for indeed, seeking first the kingdom will so prioritize one's life that every other need will be met too. (Matt. 6:33).

> "Do not worry, saying, 'What will we eat?' or 'What will we drink?' or 'What will we wear?' For it is the Gentiles who strive for all these things; and indeed your heavenly Father knows that you need all these things. But strive first for the kingdom of God and his righteousness, and all these things will be given to you as well." (Matt. 6:31-33)

Nowhere does the Bible say that the community of faith is to *build* the kingdom of God. We are invited to "see" it (Mark 9:1), "enter" it (John 3:5), "receive" it (Mark 10:15), or "proclaim" it (Luke 9:2). We are never asked to build it. The kingdom is not the work of our efforts, something we construct. The kingdom of God already exists. It is the work of God's hand. An English bishop once said that E. Stanley Jones was "obsessed with the Kingdom of God," which Jones took as a great compliment. "Would God that I were," he wrote. "It would be a magnificent obsession."[6] Jesus spoke of the kingdom more than a hundred times. Moreover, "the kingdom of God" is the only thing that Jesus ever referred to as "good news." It was the subject of his teaching and preaching, and he sent his disciples out to proclaim it everywhere.[7] Jones believed he was following Jesus' passion for the kingdom.

According to Jones, however, Jesus' emphasis on the kingdom was soon relegated to secondary importance. The disciples themselves misunderstood it when they asked to sit at his left and his right when he came into his glory (Mark 10:37). The formative creeds of the church, written two and three centuries after the Resurrection, marginalized talk of the kingdom. It is mentioned once in the Nicene Creed ("whose Kingdom shall have no end"). It is not mentioned at all in the Apostles' Creed.[8]

Perhaps some people thought Jesus' teaching on the kingdom had been restored to its rightful place and even become an earthly reality when the Roman ruler Constantine made Christianity the official religion of the empire in the year 324 CE. But as E. Stanley Jones pointed out, "The church is a relativism built more or less after the pattern of the absolute, the Kingdom of God."[9] The church can point to the kingdom of God but can never be synonymous with it. The church has too many faults. It is not that Jones did not value the church. On the contrary, he saw the church—even with all of its faults—as "the best serving institution on earth."[10] Jones believed that we need Christian community to support our ministries. We draw strength from one another in community. Moreover, our witness is diminished if we act on our faith as solitary Christians. The Christian way of being "is a way of association, of corporate living under the spirit of Jesus," Jones wrote.[11]

Jones believed that we need to recover a central emphasis on the kingdom of God. He believed that God's Order is not some fantastical dream, nor is it something only to be consummated at the end times. It is a current reality—not simply an ideal—if we would only receive it as Jesus intended and keep it at the forefront of all that we do. If as church leaders who seek a missionary mindset we can grasp the centrality of the kingdom of God as a real and livable concept, and we keep the essentials of the gospel message at the forefront of our mindset, we will be able to reach our communities with its good news and make an impact in them.

Although Jones of course knew about the kingdom of God—he had studied it and preached it—he didn't discover its power and purpose until he took a trip to Russia. There he saw the kingdom of God in a whole new way. This happened in 1934 during the depths of the Great Depression, when confidence in American capitalism was shaken to its core. Jones critiqued materialistic capitalism as a harsh system that does not distribute enough goods to all of humankind but through selfish and ruthless competition leaves people destitute. In speaking of the capitalistic system, Jones wrote, "We have become so naturalized in our insanities of hate and competition and unbrotherliness and injustice that we are afraid of the sanity of love and cooperation and brotherliness and justice."[12]

Russia, in the early 1930s, was creating a new way of ordering society through communism, although it was doing so without God. Jones was intrigued and disturbed at the same time. He was intrigued that a new world order, built on cooperation, was unfolding. But he was disturbed about Russia's atheistic foundation. He traveled to Russia to see firsthand what was happening. Jones ended up writing two books as a result of this trip, *Christ's Alternative to Communism* and *The Choice Before Us*. Both books dealt with the theme that we must decide between a materialistic, atheistic communist world and the kingdom of God on earth. Jones also saw the kingdom of God as an alternative to the mercilessness of capitalism. Jones described both communism and the kingdom of God as totalitarianisms, one built by humans, the other built by God. By taking seriously the cooperative spirit of communism, Jones drew closer to the kingdom. "I discovered the Kingdom of God in Russia," he wrote.

Russia had inwardly hit me hard. I needed reassur-
ance. In my quiet time in Moscow a verse arose out of
the Scriptures and spoke to my condition. It was this:
"Therefore let us be grateful for receiving a kingdom
that cannot be shaken" (Hebrews 12:28). "A kingdom
that cannot be shaken"—not only will not, but "cannot be shaken." I saw as in a flash that all man-made
kingdoms are shakable. The kingdom of communism is
shakable: they have to hold it together by purges, by
force; they cannot relax that force or it will fall apart.
The kingdom of capitalism is shakable. The daily fluc-
tuations of the stock market, on account of the course
of events, shows that the kingdom of capitalism is shakable. The kingdom of self is shakable. . . . Everything
is shakable, except one—the Kingdom of God, the one
and only unshakable Kingdom.[13]

Jones's discomfit with the fact that human political orders are
devoid of God, even when built on cooperation, was now reassured
by his belief in God's order—the unshakable kingdom of God that
is led by an unchanging person in Jesus Christ.

Jones framed an understanding of the kingdom of God by plac-
ing it among five kingdoms that correspond to five stages in the
development of humankind. First there is the *mineral kingdom,* and
then above that is the *plant or vegetable kingdom.* Higher yet is the
animal kingdom, then the *kingdom of humankind,* and finally the
highest of all kingdoms: *the kingdom of God.* We human beings live
between the animal kingdom and the kingdom of God. The animal
kingdom is all about self-assertion: "The weakest go to the wall
and war sounds through it," wrote Jones. "The kingdom of heaven
stands for self-sacrifice, the renewal and regeneration of the weak,
and peace and harmony and brotherhood pervade it."[14]

Jones argued that humans' position between the animal and heavenly kingdoms gives us a choice between selfishness and sacrifice. Which of the two will prevail? The higher principle of the kingdom of God helps us want to be better people, characterized more by self-sacrifice than self-assertion. We aspire to goodness and harmony rather than sinfulness and discord. The higher kingdom came down to the lower animal kingdom in the person of Jesus, who said to Nicodemus, "You must be born from above" (John 3:7). "The hope of human life," wrote Jones, "is to be born from above—the Kingdom of God. Individually and collectively, we must look up, not down"[15]

It took me a while and a lot of rereading of E. Stanley Jones to understand that he was advocating for a way of life based on receiving and living the kingdom of God—*in reality, right now!* I had dismissed talk of the kingdom as something too ideal, something to admire but impossible to live. I had grasped the eschatological import of the kingdom but dismissed its application to current events. That is, I believed that in the end times, Jesus' kingdom would be fulfilled, but that it was only an ideal, an impossible dream, for the day-to-day life of human beings.

Jones actually believed in the power of the kingdom of God to impact our lives in the here and now. Jesus said, when asked by the Pharisees when the kingdom was coming, "The kingdom of God is among you" (Luke 17:21). The kingdom is here in our midst. It is living in and among us as current reality. Jones believed that humanity yearns for order and for a leader. The order is the kingdom of God; the leader is Jesus Christ.[16]

Jones would never agree to the establishment of a human-made theocracy that would impose the kingdom on people without their choice. Such an institutionalization of the concept of the kingdom would be doomed to fail, as so many other attempts at ordering life have failed. Humankind has always fallen short of the ways of the kingdom as described in Jesus' Sermon on the Mount and parables and as embodied through his self-sacrifice. The heart of the gospel, for E. Stanley Jones, is an invitation to receive and accept Jesus, who is the leader of the kingdom of God. Receiving and accepting Jesus as Lord of one's life is at the same time a decision to live according to Jesus' order, the kingdom of God. God sent Jesus into the world for the purpose of bringing about a new world order that redeems the failed attempts of humankind to organize political structures.

We witness the failure of the human race to order the world when we experience or at least receive news daily of terrorist killings, thousands upon thousands of people forced to migrate, and the unequal distribution of resources that leads to famine, disease, and premature death. Jesus died to free us from the guilt for our complicity in a sinful world. Jesus rose from the dead to bring us newness of life. Jesus will come again to bring final and ultimate victory of the love of God over evil, death, and sin. E. Stanley Jones advocated that human beings aspire to something higher than that which was human made, that we receive the higher value of the kingdom of God and that we follow its leader, Jesus Christ. Moreover, he believed that living in such a way—as individuals and as a collective—is written into the universe. It is the way we humans were made to work—written into the very structure of all being.[17] So Jones's invitation is to accept the invitation to God's Way, the kingdom of God. When we choose this way of being, we too discover an alternative to the human-made kingdoms that tear at the fabric of life. Jones invites us to surrender these false kingdoms so we can truly embrace the kingdom of God.

SEVEN KINGDOMS TO SURRENDER

E. Stanley Jones identified seven false kingdoms that need to be surrendered if people are to be able to fully see and receive the kingdom of God. We address them in the order Jones gave in his book *Is the Kingdom of God Realism?* We remember that this book was first published in 1940. It is an indictment of humankind's inability to receive the kingdom of God that these seven items are still so evident in our world today.

1. THE KINGDOM OF RACE

If human beings are to enter into the kingdom of God, where there is no longer "Jew or Greek" (Gal. 3:28), "then we must renounce the Kingdom of Race, refuse to be governed by its presumptions and dictates, and wash our hands of its privileges and stand as a person stripped of all except one's human personality and knock at the door of the kingdom of God," wrote Jones. "Racism is built on pride, privilege and presumption. . . . There is no room in the kingdom for people who believe they belong to a superior race and must therefore have privileges."[18] The United Methodist Church compromised its integrity and witness with regard to the kingdom of race by creating a "Central Jurisdiction" in 1939 that segregated black churches from white churches into separate judicatory structures. Rather than embrace an opportunity to go beyond its default culture rooted in racism when three branches of Methodism merged together, it chose to continue the practices of race division and prejudice. Today, all churches have an opportunity to leave behind any default tendencies of racism and embrace opportunities to live in community with people of all races.

The United States, after nearly 250 years since its birth, still struggles to deal adequately with its original sin of slavery. In our efforts to reach our communities, we also keep watch that no one in our community suffers indignity at the hands of racism. We need to be proactive in bringing the values of the kingdom of God to our communities.

2. THE KINGDOM OF NATION

Anytime we human beings profess allegiance to our country above all else, we are guilty of idolatry. One's final allegiance should be to the kingdom of God. "I will give everything to my country except one thing—my conscience," wrote Jones. Jones worked tirelessly for peace. He respected those who out of strong religious conviction refused to bear arms in war. "Our country recognizes that it has no right to coerce the conscience, so it recognizes the right to be a conscientious objector." One's patriotism should not be questioned "on the ground that he is a conscientious objector. His standing is as firm as any other citizen, for a civilized State recognizes something beyond itself to which it and the individual is amenable, the kingdom of God."[19]

Jones wrote when Hitler was chancellor of Germany; Mussolini, prime minister of Italy; and Stalin, premier in the Soviet Union. There was plenty of evidence that we need to pledge allegiance to the kingdom of God over any single country. Jones never minced words about the deleterious tendencies of racism, anti-immigration, participation in war, the unfair practices that kept women from achieving their full potential as human beings, and greed in the United States of America. We are wise to measure what our country does against the precepts of the kingdom of God and to know where our ultimate allegiance lies.

3. THE KINGDOM OF THE RELIGIOUS COMMUNITY, THE CHURCH

The church is not an absolute, wrote Jones. Nor is it an end to itself. "Anyone who holds the Church first is guilty of idolatry. When the Church centers itself on itself, like the individual it loses itself. . . . One will never know the glory and beauty of the Church

155

until it is surrendered to the kingdom of God. Then it comes back to one purified and related and found. Our loyalty to our Church must bend the knee to something higher—the kingdom of God."[20]

I think Jones would agree that any religious community, including but not exclusively the church, could be held to this standard, whether the community is an expression of Islam, Buddhism, Hinduism, Judaism, or any other belief system. We live in dangerous times, when certain sects (for example, ISIS) desire to create religious states that distort the truth of the religion they profess. Christianity was guilty of such violent dominance in the age of the Crusades and the Inquisition. The individual's allegiance to God and God's kingdom must be voluntary. When it is forced on to someone, it becomes tyranny.

4. THE KINGDOM OF CLASS

Classism promotes privileges and exclusiveness based on the family in which one was born. Jones says we must surrender the kingdom of class. The kingdom of God cancels the false distinctions we humans construct claiming one economic class is better than another.[21]

In the United States, class is linked with wealth, inheritance, and race. There is a tendency to think oneself better than another if one has wealth or if one is white. Instead, if we are born into a place of wealth and privilege, we should aspire to humility and leverage such privilege to benefit others.

Jones experienced firsthand the excesses of the British class system and the injustice of the Indian caste system. Both systems attempted to put and keep poor people in their place. Any system that desires to keep people poor is incongruent with the kingdom of God, in which the righteous give food to the hungry and drink to the thirsty, welcome the stranger, clothe the naked, take care of the sick, and visit those in prison (see Matthew 25:34-36).

5. THE KINGDOM OF MONEY

When we are possessed by our possessions, we exit the kingdom of God. When money becomes the be-all and end-all of our existence, we create a whole system of values that we think are real and lasting, said Jones. We must decide whether material value or God comes first. "Possessions are all right in the hand, but wrong in the heart," wrote Jones. "They must be surrendered and placed at the disposal of the will of God."[22]

6. THE KINGDOM OF THE FAMILY

Jones wrote:

> The Kingdom of the Family must be surrendered to the Kingdom of God if it is to find itself. But the family often becomes an end in itself. Family interests decide the issues. . . . A family that lives in a state of self-reference will live in a state of self-frustration. Unless the family is dedicated to something beyond itself from which it receives goal, inspiration, and guidance, it will deteriorate into a self-centered, self-seeking unit. . . . The family is right if it is in the right place, but the right place is not the first place. When the kingdom and the family claims clash, the family claim must give way. To surrender the family may be like cutting off the right hand; but if it must be then it must be.[23]

Here Jones wanted to prioritize allegiance to the kingdom even above family. Most of the voices in my family discouraged me from accepting a call to serve in Argentina as a missionary. I took this advice kindly, as their way of saying that they would miss me and they did not want me to live far away. Ultimately, I had to make a choice, and in this case I chose to heed what I felt was a deeper calling from God and the Spirit.

7. THE KINGDOM OF THE SELF

Jones cited Matthew 16:25: "For those who want to save their life will lose it, and those who lose their life for my sake will find it." The self is to be surrendered "and lost into the will of God, and then it is found again. That self may be full of conflict and anxiety and fear and guilt when it is surrendered, but it rises from that surrender inwardly unified, with anxiety and fear gone and reconciliation and forgiveness in place of guilt."[24]

For Jones, "surrender" means that we "bend low" at the feet of Jesus and "stand straight" before everything else. "You bend before neither fear, nor sin, nor race, nor class, nor money, nor family, nor yourself. You are God's free man and woman."[25] The invitation is to so live and breathe the kingdom of God in our lives that we make it a reality.

I believe Jones's teaching on "surrender" applies to tendencies to want to control life on my own. God invites me to turn my worries and my anxieties about trying to control outcomes over to God and to let God guide me.

The invitation to church leaders is to put into practice Jesus' teaching to seek first the kingdom of God and to trust that everyday needs of this life will be added to us. This is the challenge before us as we seek a missionary mindset to reach our communities with the gospel of Jesus Christ.

THE KINGDOM AND OUR MINISTRY

Jones wrote about these false kingdoms nearly a hundred years ago, and yet they still exist. What can church leaders do today to implement a way to fully receive the kingdom that Jesus inaugurated? Here are some suggestions for those wanting to develop the missionary mindset:

1. *Follow Jesus.* Jesus did not ask people to follow his ideas; he asked us to follow him. Follow Jesus and receive the kingdom that he inaugurated with his presence and life. Keep things simple, the way E. Stanley Jones did when communicating with persons from other religious traditions: offer Jesus without the entanglements of church doctrine, church history, or denominationalism. As leaders, tell others how Jesus has made an impact in your life. Tell them of the essentials of the gospel that Christ died for us, Christ is risen, and Christ will come again. Encourage members of your community of faith to give witness to people they meet in their neighborhoods or at the workplace about how following Jesus makes a difference in their life.

2. *Believe that the kingdom is real.* Think of the kingdom of God not as a far-off dream but as something that begins right now, right here. Teach the kingdom as a real alternative to other ways of life and believe it. Remember that Jones highlighted that all humans seek order in life, and that order is the kingdom. All humans seek a leader, and that leader is Jesus Christ. The two are inextricably linked. Remember how Gandhi urged Christians not to tone down their religion or emasculate it by watering down its demands. Believe in the efficacy of the kingdom of God as a way of life.

3. *Stress cooperation.* Commit to a Christianity that is a cooperative endeavor and not something to be worked out only as individuals. In our U.S. culture we have the tendency to overemphasize the role of the individual. Remember that we are part of a team, and in our interactions work to bring witness to what we believe. Celebrate cooperative actions that make life better for people, and pay less attention to competitive actions that lift some people at the expense of others.

4. *Put generosity over greed.* Commit to "seek first the kingdom of God." Seek material things only inasmuch as they provide for your physical needs and make you mentally, spiritually, and morally fit for the purposes of the kingdom. Our U.S. culture drives people to want bigger, better, more. We are wise to remember Jesus' words that tell us not to worry so much about these material things but rather to seek first the kingdom, assuring us that "all these things will be given to you as well" (Matt. 6:33).

5. *Welcome all people.* Treat every person as if he or she were part of your own race. They are! We are all part of the human race. Celebrate the common humanity we share with others regardless of race, ethnicity, religion, sexual orientation, gender, or age. Edgehill United Methodist Church in Nashville celebrates communion every Sunday. They form a circle around the table and affirm each week: "*Everyone* has a place at this table."

6. *Study the kingdom.* Join with others to learn more about the kingdom of God. Hold one another accountable for putting the values and principles of the kingdom into practice.

Find resources about the kingdom that will help you gain a deeper understanding of its meaning. There are studies on the parables of the kingdom and on Jesus' Sermon on the Mount that can help groups plumb the depths of meaning to the values, principles, and demands of the kingdom of God. Find others to help you uncover its riches.

7. *Don't confine the kingdom to the church.* While surely the church serves as a sign of the kingdom of God, recognize others outside of Christianity who are also implementing its values and principles. At the same time, strive to work cooperatively with Christian forces by working toward Christian unity. We are to look to the kingdom of God for guidance on living our individual and corporate lives. When we see those same values lived out in others who belong to different tribes, even different religions, we should celebrate and embrace them. John Wesley called this the "catholic spirit," which puts aside differences that don't matter and embraces what we affirm together.

The invitation to church leaders who seek to have a missionary mindset is to put into practice Jesus' teaching to seek first the kingdom of God and to trust that all the other things we need will be added to us. This is the challenge before us as we seek to reach our communities with the gospel of Jesus Christ.

YOUR TURN:
QUESTIONS FOR REFLECTION AND DISCUSSION

1. Describe times when you have experienced weariness and hopelessness in the face of world problems.

2. What do you think of E. Stanley Jones's notion that the kingdom of God is realism?

3. What "kingdoms" must be surrendered today so people can fully embrace living in and receiving the kingdom of God?

4. What is the role of the church in serving as a catalyst of the kingdom of God?

9

TRUST

BELIEVING IN AND LIVING BY THE POWER AND TRUTH OF THE GOSPEL

Trust in the LORD with all your heart,
and do not rely on your own insight.
In all your ways acknowledge him,
and he will make straight your paths.
—PROVERBS 3:5-6

I remember when my colleague and supervisor, Hugo Urcola, returned from the funeral of Adam Sosa on the last day of November 1983. "People were smiling as they told stories about Adam," said Hugo. "There was laughter and joy and peace."

Adam was a faithful ministerial servant of the church. He grew up as the son of a Methodist pastor and followed his father in the same calling. He served churches not only in Argentina, but also in Montevideo, Uruguay. He taught the history of the church at the Methodist seminary of Buenos Aires, helped found a confederation of Protestant churches that served Argentina and Uruguay, and had a regular radio program called *The Evangelical Voice*. Upon retiring from the pastorate, he was able to dedicate more time to his passion, translation, and he translated hundreds of books and articles from English, French, Italian, and Portuguese to Spanish. The list included Roland Allen's *The Spontaneous Expansion of the Church*, in 1970.[1] He served as the copresident of the Argentine Fellowship for Christians and Jews.[2] His son, Pablo, is a renowned church musician who has led choirs and congregations across the world, including at gatherings of the World Council of Churches. Those present at the funeral included Bishops Pagura and Gattinoni, superintendents Aldo Etchegoyen and Hugo Urcola, and many pastors and lay leaders from across the church. A quiet confidence in the truth of the gospel emanated from these leaders of the Evangelical Methodist Church in Argentina.

I listened intently as Hugo shared about the funeral service. Adam had lived a good and long life and had been faithful in every way to God and the church. In the Methodist tradition, we call funerals "services of death and resurrection." In this context of church leaders and friends who shared a common faith and had dedicated their lives to living out the gospel of Jesus Christ, the service was even more. It was a celebration.

It was a celebration because of a shared conviction among most of the people attending. While there was sadness at Adam's parting, there was much more joy, because he had lived life to the fullest and had embraced as much as any person can what it means to live under the guidance of the kingdom of God and to follow Jesus. The words of Jesus rang true when applied to Adam: "Well done, good and faithful servant!" (Matt. 25:23 NIV).

I don't remember everything that Hugo shared with me about Adam's funeral. I do remember the picture he painted of a serene and confident group of people gathered to celebrate a life and say farewell to a good and faithful servant. The confidence sprang from lives surrendered to a power greater than themselves. A quiet power of love and goodness permeated the air. These were ordinary human beings who had been brought to a higher level of existence because of their rootedness in the way of living exemplified by Jesus. They faced the same trials and temptations that all humans face, but they faced them in the context of a faith solid and firm. This confidence rooted in the gospel is trust. We *so* trust ourselves to God and *so* align ourselves with God's kingdom that peace enters our innermost being, and we can live with calm serenity, even in the face of death.

The picture Hugo painted of that funeral was one I wanted to be in. I would have characterized myself as being on the way toward what they seemed to firmly have. These Christian leaders I knew and loved had surrounded me long enough that I recognized their strength. I longed for that strength and confidence rooted in faith. I aspired to the serenity and peace exuded by these followers of Jesus. I was thankful that they had given me a glimpse, a taste, of what life could be when one surrenders fully to the kingdom that Jesus inaugurated with his presence and person. This was a faith that remained confident in the face of national calamity (disappearances, war with Great Britain, economic instability) and that could look into the face of death and be serene, at peace, even celebrative.

The example of church leaders in Argentina solidified my faith and cemented my decision to commit myself to a lifelong ministry as a member of the kingdom of God that Jesus led. Hearing the story of Adam Sosa's funeral crystallized for me that I had chosen the right path in coming to Argentina. They were teaching me so much. I learned what it was like to be part of a "minority religion." Roman Catholicism was the dominant Christian denomination in the country. Pentecostalism had gained many adherents before and during my time living in the country. Those of us who belonged to what was called "the historical Protestant traditions" (Methodist, Lutheran, Presbyterian, Anglican, or Episcopalian, Reformed) were a small percentage of the overall Christian population. The Evangelical Methodist Church of Argentina was composed of only ten thousand adherents in one hundred churches dispersed over a vast geography of provinces.

I learned to value being part of a smaller expression of God's universal church. While we were small in number, our voice carried far because of the courage of leaders like Bishop Gattinoni, Bishop Pagura, soon-to-be Bishop Etchegoyen, and countless voices of laity and clergy from local churches around the country who were not afraid to speak out against the violation of human rights occurring during the so-called Dirty War against subversion.

I learned that our platform, though small, was nevertheless powerful. Adam's son, Pablo, demonstrates that power. He brought inspired music and liturgy to Christians around the world, introducing new Christian songs with the beat and rhythm of the Andes as well as the cities of South America (milonga, tango) at large ecumenical gatherings. This one leader from a small denomination in Argentina had a platform that reached thousands of people. A song that Pablo helped popularize around Latin America and beyond was one that Bishop Pagura penned during the difficult times living under military dictatorship. Pagura wrote the lyrics of "Tenemos Esperanza" ("We have hope") to a tango melody Homero Perera composed.[3] In the midst of one of the bleakest periods in Argentina's and Latin America's history, when people "disappeared" and human rights were violated, he wrote about hope. "We have hope," the song goes in its English translation, "because He [Jesus] entered into the world and history and because He broke the silence of agony, because he filled the earth with his glory; because he was light in our cold night . . . because

He sowed love and life; because He broke hardened hearts and lifted up depressed souls . . ."[4]

I learned that Christians could play an important role as the conscience of a country. It is a delicate calling. When a Christian church speaks out against the abuse of human rights, the mistreatment of indigenous peoples, inequities that make life more difficult for the poor, it will be accused of playing partisan politics. E. Stanley Jones received such accusations during his lifetime. "Stanley Jones is a modernist," was a frequent accusation, which would translate today as being too "liberal." Jones said that he was neither a fundamentalist nor a modernist, but rather a "Christian in the making."[5] I witnessed in the Argentine leaders a great ability to use their voice in ways that were nonpartisan—unless you consider the words of the Bible a partisan point of view, partisan toward the kingdom.

I learned most of all the importance of trusting the gospel, trusting God. E. Stanley Jones said, "Self-surrender is the way out of being what we are into being what we might be and ought to be."[6] This surrender of self flows out of our understanding of and response to the essential message of the gospel that Christ died for us, Christ is risen for our renewal, and Christ will come again in final victory over the forces of evil. Jones's vocation was evangelist. He ended most sermons with an invitation for people to surrender—to come to the altar and "lay at the feet of Christ" and to trust God and follow Jesus. "I believe the Spirit of God is here," he said at the conclusion of a sermon on grace preached in 1954. "And He is doing the urging and you are going to listen to His urging and to your own inner urges and I believe that you will come."[7]

We are called to find ways to extend the invitation of the gospel today. It is vital to keep a balanced witness, addressing issues of social injustice, racism, unfair treatment of women—issues that

Jones addressed—even as we remember our primary task to invite people into a relationship with God through Jesus Christ.

LEARNING TO TRUST

I learned an important lesson about trusting God rather than myself during my first term as a missionary. While living in Dolores, Argentina, we drove an old hand-me-down car that had been given to the congregation by a faithful member of the English-speaking church in Buenos Aires. This 1963 Peugeot was sixteen years old when I received it. It was good transportation and totally unpretentious. Many who met me and learned that I was a fraternal worker from the United States expected me to drive a late-model car. Not only could I not afford to drive a late-model car; I enjoyed driving this old clunker, which was very affordable. I liked the car, and I learned later from friends that being seen in it broke the stereotype of the wealthy foreign missionary driving the new-model vehicle.

While driving to one of the preaching points outside of Dolores, I heard a distinct *clunk, clunk, clunk* coming from the engine. Somehow, I learned later, the oil had been blocked from lubricating the pistons, and I found myself with a blown engine. I turned the car around and managed to drive to a car repair shop to see what could be done. The mechanic said he would have to take the engine apart and rebore the pistons, putting in new gaskets. The cost was high, more than we could afford. But we needed the car to reach two distant preaching points and decided to trust that we would find the money somehow, so we gave the go-ahead for the mechanic to start work.

The car died in December, a time when Christmas cards came in the mail from families and friends in the United States. Just three days into the car repair, we received a card from a family who had been members of our church back in Bergen County, New Jersey. In addition to giving Christmas greetings, the card included a check with a note in the card that said, "We have had an exceptionally good year in business and wanted to pass on this blessing to you." Once you converted the amount of the check from dollars to pesos, it turned out to be almost exactly what the repair was to cost. I don't know how to explain those kinds of experiences except to say it has something to do with having faith and trusting God.

E. Stanley Jones lived his life trusting God. His deep prayer life opened him up to listening to what God was saying to him. Many times Jones talked of how he listened to the Voice that led him to obey the guidance of the Spirit in his life. It was this "Voice" that led him to discover his special calling of reaching out to the higher castes in India. I admit that I am leery whenever someone says that he or she gets messages directly from God, but I found Jones's explanation of how it worked for him helpful. Jones says that he questions whenever someone glibly says, "God said this to me." That is being too slick, wrote Jones. Still, he believed that God can guide us through an "inner voice" that comes to us. He was not referring to something audible, but to words that come together in our minds when we meditate or talk to ourselves.

For Jones, it is very important to distinguish between our own subconscious talking to us and the voice of God giving us a message. The former tries to convince us of something, as if we are arguing with ourselves. The voice of God, however, "does not argue, does not try to convince you. It just speaks."[8] It wells up inside and cannot be ignored. For example, Jones heard the Voice tell him to stay in the United States during the summer of 1941, rather than return to India. He discerned that there was a purpose to staying and that it had to do with his attempted intervention to avoid war between Japan and the United States. Jones said that he did not rely exclusively on the inner voice for guidance and admitted that it would have been dangerous to do so. "For if you depend on the inner voice almost exclusively, you are likely to manufacture that voice from the subconscious and call it the voice of God."[9] In fact, Jones admitted that on two occasions he mistook his subconscious voice for the voice of God. "In both cases the voice turned out wrong." He was wary of the voice after those incidents and always sought to make sure that the voice that was speaking to him was not arguing but rather making a statement to follow.[10]

Whenever confronted with a dilemma or a difficult choice, Jones would meditate and wait upon a word from God. He observed that when we surrender the self to God, we let go of the anxious work of trying to control things and outcomes, and we instead live out the true meaning of comfort: "*com*, meaning with, and *fortis*, meaning strength—strengthened by being with another. You are strengthened with all the power of the higher Power," wrote Jones. "It is a transfusion that makes us become a transformed person, different—doing things that you can't do and going places that you can't go and being what you can't be."[11]

Hugo's story of the funeral of Adam Sosa helped me put many things in perspective for my own faith journey. If these church leaders from the Evangelical Methodist Church in Argentina could face death with such peace and serenity, this was the place for me. Death was not the final word for Adam or the attendees at his celebrative service. They could trust that in God's hands, Adam would be forever safe, and they too would be when they breathed their last. So would I when I breathed my last.

Such trust, such faith, stood in stark contrast to those who lived without any relationship with God. As a pastor, I was called upon to conduct funerals. Sometimes I was called by a funeral parlor working with a family that specifically wanted a Protestant pastor to conduct the service, but sometimes the deceased had no relationship to a community of faith. When I conducted funerals for members of the church, I experienced a similar sense of calm and serenity that Hugo had described at Adam Sosa's service. The funerals of nonmembers felt different for me. I always tried to console the family and tried to learn as much as I could about the deceased loved one. I always wanted to provide words of hope. However, the traditional words of the funeral rite would not ring true as they did for faithful followers of Jesus who had been part of a community of faith.

I was never given the opportunity to offer any words at all for a burial that took place in Dolores, one that was held in silence. Those services felt altogether sad and lonely. A young member of the church, Marcelo, asked me to help out when his cousin had died suddenly. His twenty-one-year-old cousin had been a jockey rider and fell off his horse during a race and was trampled to death. Marcelo introduced me to the jockey's family at the funeral parlor. I expressed the deep condolences of our church family and offered to help in any way.

Marcelo asked his family if I could say a prayer at the wake or at the funeral to be held the next day. They told him that they did not want any words. I respected their decision. I was, after all, a stranger to them. I was there because of Marcelo, and I accompanied him throughout the wake and the burial. But the service was a burial, not a funeral, because there were no words spoken. Family and friends processed in a caravan of cars from the funeral parlor to the cemetery. His coffin was carted from the hearse to the niche in a corner of the cemetery. No one from the family said any words. There were silence and tears. Hopelessness hung in the air.

How very different from the serenity of Adam Sosa's funeral and the many other funerals I conducted for those who were part of our community of faith. The contrast had everything to do with faith and trust. When the person who has died believed in something greater than himself, then death does not have the last word. Words can be spoken that bring hope despite the despair of having lost a loved one. I am grateful that in my life I have been surrounded by a community of believers that I can call "family." That family now includes people from my home country and from other countries and places where my path has crossed the paths of other believers and we have connected with each other. This belonging, this peace, this serenity in the face of death, and this pathway for life guided by God provide the foundation for hope. This faith and trust in the unshakable kingdom and the unchanging person of Jesus provides a way forward for life.

It was this ultimate trust in the providence of God that held sway for E. Stanley Jones. He could take part in honest dialogue with people of other faiths at the roundtable, because he trusted the Spirit of God to reveal truth in the proceedings. He asked the religious leaders from various religious communities and the skeptics "not to argue or try to make a case, but rather tell what they had actually found in religious experience."[12] The facts, he trusted, would throw people into the arms of Christ. He didn't rely on himself for the success or failure of the roundtable. He trusted God.

When one watches videos of E. Stanley Jones preaching, even as an older man, he clearly and boldly conveys his confidence in the gospel of Jesus Christ. One of his favorite books that he wrote was *The Way*, and he lived his life and preached the good news that Jesus' way was "the Way." He was convicted of the truth of Jesus' Way. He trusted completely that we need to surrender ourselves to the unshakable kingdom led by the unchanging Christ. He learned about other religions, so that he could contrast their beliefs with Christian beliefs, but he did so with respect and honesty and love.

Roland Allen advocated that we put our trust in the Holy Spirit when we go about planting new ministries for new people in new places. He urged the church to let loose the controls that often impede the development of communities of faith. If only we could trust more completely that God's Spirit would work in and among us in such a way that the new believers we encountered could, in a short period of time, begin to lead the movement themselves.

IMAGINE THE IMPACT

I think there are relevant "take-aways" from the lives and teachings of E. Stanley Jones and Roland Allen that can help church leaders who desire a missionary mindset to reach their communities with the gospel of Jesus Christ.

Christians with a missionary mindset approach a community as if we ourselves were from some foreign land. We don't assume anything about the community, even if we were born there and grew up there. We start with a clean slate. We reflect on our "default culture"—our own upbringing and the biases and understandings that up until now we may have taken for granted. We cultivate an awareness of this default, so we recognize when we interpret our experience while wearing the tinted glass of our particular past and when our past even blinds us from seeing other perspectives.

Christians with a missionary mindset seek ways to embrace the cultures of others. We want to take in the aromas and the sights and the sounds and the promise and the possibility of other ways of understanding the world: its food, clothing, language, slang, hurts, hopes, art, music, stories. In these times, we need people of all races and nationalities to serve as instruments of God's kingdom to bring people together in community. In our churches and in our community organizations, we should seek to break down ethnic and religious barriers, so we can meet each other as human beings—gifts of God.

With a missionary mindset, we fall to our knees in prayer before embarking on knowing our community, for we know that our own gifts and talents, however sharp they may be, fall short of perfect love. We pray that God guide us and those who work with us to open our hearts and minds that we can listen deeply, love unconditionally, and trust the movement of the Spirit in our midst.

As Christians with a missionary mindset, we seek a greater understanding of ourselves. Not only do we want to gain an awareness of our default culture, but we want to cultivate a deeper self-awareness of who we are. Knowing ourselves better and gaining clarity about our own strengths and weaknesses and our own personality type will help us build bridges of love and understanding to the people we seek to reach. Our self-awareness will help us draw upon our strengths. It will also help us understand our weaknesses, so we can try to surround ourselves with people who have complementary gifts. Self-awareness can help us recognize the difference between the individuals we were taught to be (our default) and the individuals we are trying to become in Christ.

With a missionary mindset, we recognize that the only way we can even begin to deepen our understanding of the people in our community is by listening deeply; that is, listening beyond the words that are shared in conversation and connecting to the stories of the people. We listen with our ears and we listen with our hearts and we seek to understand.

As people with a missionary mindset, we acknowledge that our approach, if it should have a chance to be received well, will be characterized by humility. It is not a false humility that wants to be noticed. Rather, it is a humility born in the soul of a follower of Jesus who wants the very best for others. It is a humility that does not seek acclaim but rather gives all the glory and honor to God for any success, any spark of hope that comes about.

While we want to cultivate prayer, self-awareness, and humility for our missionary mindset, more than anything we want to love. We are ever mindful—as the Peter Scholtes song conveys—that they will know we are Christians by our love,[13] and we aspire to the *agape* love that Jesus exemplified and that Paul described in his first letter to the Corinthians.

Roland Allen taught us that with a missionary mindset, we plant churches the way Paul did in the early church. Whether we are denominational leaders or church planters, we are urged to follow Paul's lead and make church planting not so much about our efforts at control, but about following the lead of the Holy Spirit. It is about communicating the essentials of the gospel clearly to people, so they know and embrace that Christ died for us; Christ is risen for us; and that Christ will come again. It is about training up those who join our new communities of faith, so they can take on leadership roles. Like Paul, while we stay in contact and make periodic visits, we work ourselves out of a job as soon as possible.

A missionary mindset strives for the kingdom of God. E. Stanley Jones gave a balanced Christian witness. In addition to calling people to give their lives to the unchanging Savior, Jesus Christ, he also called hearers to enter into the unshakable kingdom that Jesus proclaimed, a kingdom of peace, of love, of cooperation with others. Jones was an evangelist who not only made altar calls, but called on the president of the United States to advocate for peace. He called on people in the United States to rid themselves of racism. He lifted up the importance of women taking leadership roles not only in the church but in all of life. The fact that he advocated for such social justice seventy and eighty years ago should catch our attention as we continue to find ways forward on these issues today.

E. Stanley Jones always referred to himself as a "Christian in the making." For as much as he knew the way of Christ and the way of the gospel, he also was humble enough to know that he did not live out the Christian life in all its perfect fullness. As we strive to incorporate all of these principles into our lives and witness when we reach out to our communities, we, too, know that we are still Christians in the making.

As imperfect as we are on this journey of faith, however, we can move forward with confidence because we trust God. That trust allows us to imagine a different world, a world that E. Stanley Jones saw as replacing this present, unworkable world order, based on greed and selfishness, with God's order. We imagine a world where hope trumps fear. We imagine a world where respect and civility characterize our dialogue with people of other faiths and with those who profess no faith at all. We imagine leaders of communities of faith serving as peacemakers. We imagine churches championing cooperation over competition. We imagine people of faith embracing others of differing races as brothers and sisters. We imagine vast teams of disciples transforming their communities through the love of God. We imagine a world filled with those who would receive the unshakable kingdom and follow the unchanging Jesus.

YOUR TURN:
QUESTIONS FOR REFLECTION AND DISCUSSION

1. What about a Christian funeral demonstrates trust in God?

2. Who have you seen demonstrate complete trust in God?

3. When have you seen the tension between "controlling" the mission of the church and "following the Spirit" in Christian mission?

4. How can a missionary mindset help you reach your community with the gospel of Jesus Christ?

SMALL GROUP STUDY GUIDE

A *Missionary Mindset* is an invitation to church leaders to rediscover principles that will help us reach out to our communities with the gospel. The questions in the "Your Turn" section at
the end of each chapter are designed to help guide a small group
from the local church through a process of discernment, reflection,
and discovery. It is our hope that this group will uncover a fresh
vision for the mission to which God invites them.

These suggestions for small group study are designed to be
a resource for local church leaders. There are ten sessions that
correspond directly to the introduction and nine chapters of *A*
Missionary Mindset. When, how long, and how often the team will
meet will need to be decided by the group itself.

It is our prayer that, through the study of this book, local church
leaders will be drawn more closely together and will become the
leaven that will help their entire church reach their community
more effectively.

Each session is formatted the same. Follow the outline of a typ-
ical session here. The particular scripture lesson(s) for each session is listed for the chapter studied.

Agenda for each session:
    Opening prayer
    Scripture reading

Discussion

1. Assign someone to take notes on behalf of the group. Keep a running log of notes so that the group can refer to comments and insights throughout the study period.
2. Respond to the questions in the "Your Turn" section at the end of the chapter.
3. Assign reading for the next session.

Closing prayer

INTRODUCTION: Matthew 28:16-20; Acts 15:1-31; 1 Corinthians 9:19-22; Galatians 2:11-14

CHAPTER 1: Matthew 22:37-39; Colossians 3:12-17

CHAPTER 2: Colossians 1:9-14; 1 Thessalonians 5:12-22

CHAPTER 3: 2 Peter 1:5-7

CHAPTER 4: John 4:6-30

CHAPTER 5: Matthew 23:11-12; Philippians 2:1-11

CHAPTER 6: John 13:31-35; 1 Corinthians 13

CHAPTER 7: Acts 16:1-15; 18:1-4: 1 Thessalonians 2:9-12

CHAPTER 8: Matthew 5:1-12; 6:31-33; Hebrews 12:28

CHAPTER 9: Proverbs 3:1-10; Matthew 25:31-46

APPENDIX

Supplemental Resources for *A Missionary Mindset*

E. STANLEY JONES BOOKS IN PRINT

Abundant Living: 364 Daily Devotions, foreword by Leonard Sweet (Nashville: Abingdon, 2014). Available in paperback and e-book formats.

The Christ of the Indian Road (Nashville: Abingdon Press, 2010). Available in paperback and e-book formats.

How to Pray, with commentary by Tom Albin (Nashville: Upper Room Books, 2015). Available in paperback and e-book formats.

Anne Mathews-Younes, *Living upon the Way: Selected Sermons of E. Stanley Jones on Self Surrender and Conversion* (United Christian Ashrams, 2008).

A Song of Ascents: A Spiritual Autobiography, foreword by James K. Mathews (Nashville: Abingdon Press, 1968).

The Way: 364 Daily Devotions (Nashville: Abingdon Press, 2015). Available in paperback and e-book formats.

The Word Became Flesh (Nashville: Abingdon Press, 2006).

Victorious Living: 364 Daily Devotions, foreword by Leonard Sweet (Nashville: Abingdon Press, 2014). Available in paperback and e-book formats.

Out-of-print copies of books by E. Stanley Jones can be found through Amazon.com, eBay, and Half.com, among other online bookstores.

RESOURCES FOR SELF-AWARENESS

DiSC Profile: https://www.onlinediscprofile.com/

The Myers-Briggs Type Indicator: http://www.myersbriggs.org/my-mbti-personality-type/take-the-mbti-instrument/

Strength Finders: a product of the Gallup Organization: https://www.gallupstrengthscenter.com/?gclid=Cj0KEQiAkIWzBRDK1ayo-Yjt38wBEiQAi7NnP4l9-nSTOfgEVkJ8R-z75AbO9ls7BWEEZBHqzPMG21QaAi_M8P8HAQ

IDI (Intercultural Development Inventory), which measures cross-cultural competencies: https://idiinventory.com/

For Church Planter Candidate Assessments:

- Lifeway: http://churchplanter.lifeway.com/
- Path 1 online assessment: http://www.umcdiscipleship.org/new-church-starts/assessment; for the Spanish-language assessment, click on the "Español" tab

NOTES

Introduction

1. I am indebted to an article written by Mark D. Nanos for insights into how the apostle Paul navigated the boundary waters of sharing the gospel across cultures. See Mark D. Nanos, "Paul and Judaism," in *The Jewish Annotated New Testament*, ed. Amy-Jill Levine and Marc Zvi Brettler (New York: Oxford University Press, 2011), 551–54.
2. Stephen Neill, *A History of Christian Missions*, 2nd ed. (London and New York: Penguin, 1986), 143.
3. Diana Butler Bass, *A People's History of Christianity: The Other Side of the Story* (San Francisco: HarperOne, 2009), 7.
4. George Barna and David Kinnaman, gen. eds., *Churchless: Understanding Today's Unchurched and How to Connect with Them* (n.p.: Barna: 2014).

Chapter 1

1. "ESJ Foundation Interviews," YouTube video, 8:29, from an interview of Len Sweet, posted by the E. Stanley Jones Foundation on July 25, 2012, https://www.youtube.com/watch?v=FjeV2EUG8_g.
2. E. Stanley Jones, *The Christ of the American Road* (New York: Abingdon-Cokesbury Press, 1944), 15.
3. For 1962, see "Nomination Database," Nobelprize.org, accessed February 1, 2016, http://www.nobelprize.org/nomination/archive/show.php?id=17004; and for 1963 by eleven members of the Swedish Parliament, see "Nomination Database," Nobelprize.org, accessed February 1, 2016, http://www.nobelprize.org/nomination/archive/show.php?id=17156.

4. Jones, *The Christ of the American Road*, 180.
5. A new edition of this book was published by Abingdon in 2014.
6. E. Stanley Jones, *The Christ of the Indian Road* (New York: Abingdon, 1925), 22; emphasis added.
7. Ibid.
8. Ibid.
9. Ibid., 21.
10. Ibid., 23.
11. Ibid., 24.
12. Jones described this in his book *Christ at the Round Table* (New York: Abingdon, 1928).
13. Jones, *The Christ of the Indian Road*, 26.
14. Ibid., 28.
15. Ibid., 31.
16. Ibid., 30.
17. Cathy Lynn Grossman, "Christians Lose Ground, 'Nones' Soar in New Portrait of US Region," Religious News Service, May 12, 2015, http://www.religionnews.com/2015/05/12/christians-lose-ground -nones-soar-new-portrait-u-s-religion/?utm_medium=email&utm _campaign=RNS+Daily+Report+–+Tuesday+May+12+2015&utm_ content=RNS+Daily+Report+--+Tuesday+May+12+2015+CID_ 2112e9db39f3016b96251aed7349a790&utm_source=Campaign%20 Monitor&utm_term=VIEW%20STORY%20AT%20WWW RELIGIONNEWSCOM.
18. Jones, *Christ at the Round Table*, 23.
19. Ibid.

Chapter 2

1. E. Stanley Jones, *How to Pray* (Nashville: Upper Room Books, 2015), 45.
2. Rueben P. Job and Norman Shawchuck, eds., *A Guide to Prayer for Ministers and Other Servants* (Nashville: Upper Room, 1983).
3. Carlo Carretto, *The God Who Comes* (n.p.: Orbis, 1974); *I Sought and I Found: My Experience of God and of the Church* (n.p.: Orbis, 1984); *Letters from the Desert* (n.p.: Orbis, 1972); *I, Francis* (Maryknoll, NY: Orbis, 1982).

4. Jones, *How to Pray*, 21–23.

5. Ibid., 21.

6. E. Stanley Jones, *Victorious Living*, repr. (Nashville: Abingdon, 2015), 60.

7. Ibid., 245.

8. Consider using the web community Moyo (http://www.moyoliving .org/), which provides online avenues to post reflections and to bridge the gap between contemplation and action.

9. See http://www.commontexts.org/rcl/ for more information and to download the readings.

10. Jones, *Victorious Living*, 244.

11. The following description of *Lectio Divina* is used with permission from the Upper Room's *Alive Now* magazine, Beth Richardson, managing editor.

Chapter 3

1. A third assessment tool, especially geared for church planters, is offered by Lifeway Christian Resources. For more information and the online assessment tool, go to the Church Planter Candidate Assessment page at http://churchplanter.lifeway.com/ (accessed February 1, 2016).

2. For more information, visit the Online DiSC Profile website at https://www.onlinediscprofile.com/.

3. Isabel Briggs Meyers, the Myers & Briggs Foundation website, accessed February 1, 2016, http://www.myersbriggs.org /myers-and-briggs-foundation/objectives-and-mission/.

4. For more information about the Kaleidoscope Institute and the ministry of the Reverend Eric H. F. Law, see http://www.kscopeinstitute .org/ (accessed February 1, 2016).

5. "History of the Kaleidoscope Institute," accessed February 1, 2016, http://www.kscopeinstitute.org/about-1/.

6. Eric H. F. Law, *The Wolf Shall Dwell with the Lamb: Spirituality for Leadership in a Multicultural Community* (n.p.: Chalice Press, 1993), 82.

7. Ibid.

Chapter 4

1. *Webster's Third New International Dictionary of the English Language, Unabridged*, s.v. "presence."
2. Sherry Turkle, "Stop Googling. Let's Talk: What Have We Done to Face-to-Face Conversation?," *New York Times Sunday Review*, September 27, 2015, http://www.nytimes.com/2015/09/27/opinion /sunday/stop-googling-lets-talk.html.
3. For a discussion on family and divorce, see "Jewish Family Life in the First Century CE," in *The Jewish Annotated New Testament*, ed. Amy-Jill Levine and Marc Zvi Brettler (Oxford: Oxford University Press, 2011), 537–40.
4. Erica Allen served as a Path1 Resident 2014–15. She learned at the feet of Pastor Jacob Armstrong of Providence UMC in Mount Juliet, Tennessee, in preparation for starting a new church in East Nashville. I was blessed to be asked to join her launch team in the spring of 2015.

Chapter 5

1. For a thorough exposition of Borges's English ancestors, see Martín Hadis, *Literatos y Excéntricos: Los Ancestros Ingleses de Jorge Luis Borges* (Buenos Aires: Editorial Sudamericana, 2006).
2. For more information, see the website of Vanderbloemen Search Group, accessed February 2, 2016, at http://www.vanderbloemen.com/.
3. William Vanderbloemen, "5 Leadership Lessons from Pope Francis," *Fast Company*, September 15, 2015. http://www.fastcompany.com /3051514/know-it-all/5-lessons-every-leader-can-learn-from-pope -francis?partner=themost&utm_source=themost&utm_medium=link.
4. Ibid.
5. Ibid.
6. Ibid.
7. Ibid.
8. Ibid.
9. Stephen Cherry, *Barefoot Disciple: Walking the Way of Passionate Humility* (London: Continuum, 2011), 39.
10. Ibid., 42.
11. John H. Sammis (1846–1919), "Trust and Obey," *United Methodist Hymnal*, no. 467, http://www.hymnsite.com/lyrics/umh467.sht.

Chapter 6

1. Mahatma Gandhi, quoted in E. Stanley Jones, *Gandhi: Portrayal of a Friend* (Nashville: Abingdon, 1948), 51.
2. E. Stanley Jones, *The Christ of the Indian Road* (New York: Abingdon, 1925), 110.
3. U.S. Department of State, Office of the Historian, "The Immigration Act of 1924 (The Johnson-Reed Act)" on the web page MILESTONES: 1921–1936, accessed February 2, 2016, https://history.state.gov /milestones/1921-1936/immigration-act.
4. Jones, *Indian Road*, 117.
5. Ibid., 112.
6. Ibid., 51–52.
7. Anne Schindler, "Fla. 'Sex Offender Village' becomes refuge for the reviled," First Coast News, n.d., http://www.firstcoastnews.com /story/news/local/florida/2015/02/05/sex-offender-refuge-pahokee /22928913/.
8. Ibid.
9. Ibid.
10. E. Stanley Jones, *The Way to Power and Poise* (Nashville: Abingdon, 1949), 163.
11. Ibid., 166.
12. Kenneth Johnson, "Demographic Trends in Rural and Small Town America," *Reports on Rural America* 1, no. 1 (Durham, NH: Carsey Institute, University of New Hampshire, 2006), executive summary, http://scholars.unh.edu/cgi/viewcontent.cgi?article=1004&context =carsey.
13. E. Stanley Jones, *Victorious Living* (Nashville: Abingdon, 2015), 321.
14. For more information about the Missional Wisdom Academy, see the Missional Wisdom Foundation website (accessed February 2, 2016) at http://missionalwisdom.com/academy/overview/.

Chapter 7

1. Roland Allen, *The Spontaneous Expansion of the Church and the Causes Which Hinder It*, (Eugene, OR: Wipf and Stock, 1962), 6.
2. Roland Allen, *Missionary Methods: St. Paul's or Ours?* with a foreword by Lesslie Newbigin (Grand Rapids: Eerdmans, 1962).

3. See "Collection Level Description: Papers of the United Society for the Propagation of the Gospel," on the website of the Bodleian Library, University of Oxford, accessed February 2, 2016, http://www.bodley .ox.ac.uk/dept/scwmss/wmss/online/blcas/uspg.html.

4. J. D. Payne, "The Legacy of Roland Allen," *Churchman*, n.d., http://church society.org/docs/churchman/117/Cman_117_4_Payne.pdf, 318–19.

5. Ibid., 319.

6. Rick Warren, *The Purpose Driven Church: Growth Without Compromising Your Message and Mission* (Grand Rapids: Zondervan, 1995), 285.

7. Kenneth Jeffrey Nash, *The Identifying, Equipping, and Sending of Laypersons to Lead a Multi-Site Church* (Wilmore, KY: Asbury Theological Seminary, 2014); available online at http://place.asbury seminary.edu/cgi/viewcontent.cgi?article=1805&context=ecommon satsdissertations.

8. Roger Finke and Rodney Stark, "How the Upstart Sects Won America: 1776–1850," *Journal for the Scientific Study of Religion* 28, no. 1 (1989): 27, quoted in Nash, 28.

9. Allen, *The Spontaneous Expansion of the Church*, 8.

10. Ibid.

11. Paul Grant, "The Three Self Movement in China," Urbana[15] blog, October 18, 2011, https://urbana.org/blog/three-self-patriotic -movement-china.

12. Tom Phillips, "China on course to become 'world's most Christian nation' within 15 years, *Telegraph* (UK), December 5, 2015, http://www .telegraph.co.uk/news/worldnews/asia/china/10776023/China-on -course-to-become-worlds-most-Christian-nation-within-15-years .html.

13. Allen, *Missionary Methods*, 51–52.

14. Tim Weeks, "La Luz de Cristo crece y crece: un modelo a seguir," *El Interprete*, September–October 2012, http://hispanic.umc.org/news /la-luz-de-cristo-crece-y-crece-un-modelo-a-seguir. Translated by Douglas Ruffle.

15. Allen, *Missionary Methods*, 84.

16. See Stephen R. Covey, *The 7 Habits of Highly Effective People: Powerful Lessons in Personal Change*, 25th anniv. ed. (New York: Simon & Schuster, 2013), pt. 2, Habit 2.

17. Allen, *Missionary Methods*, 55.

Chapter 8

1. E. Stanley Jones, *A Song of Ascents: A Spiritual Autobiography* (Nashville: Abingdon, 1968), 153.

2. Paul H. Lewis, *Guerrillas and Generals: The "Dirty War" in Argentina* (Westport, CT: Praeger, 2002), 150.

3. *Nunca Más (Never Again)*: A Report by Argentina's National Commission on Disappeared People (London: Faber and Faber, 1986), 11.

4. Nelly Ritchie, in *Iglesias Evangélicas y Derechos Humanos en la Argentina (1976–1998)*, by Pablo Andiñach and Daniel Bruno (Ediciones La Aurora, 2001); translated by Douglas Ruffle, 145.

5. See "The Wesleyan Means of Grace," website of the United Methodist Church, accessed February 2, 2016, http://www.umc.org/how-we -serve/the-wesleyan-means-of-grace.

6. E. Stanley Jones, *A Song of Ascents*, 152–53.

7. Ibid.

8. Ibid.

9. E. Stanley Jones, *Is the Kingdom of God Realism?* (New York: Abingdon-Cokesbury, 1940), 63.

10. E. Stanley Jones, *The Way* (n.p.: 1946), 309.

11. Ibid.

12. E. Stanley Jones, *Christ's Alternative to Communism* (New York: Abingdon-Cokesbury, 1951), 61.

13. Jones, *The Way*, 149–50.

14. E. Stanley Jones, *Christ at the Round Table* (New York: Abingdon, 1928), 71.

15. Jones, *Is the Kingdom of God Realism?* 200.

16. Jones, *The Way*, 64.

17. Jones, *Is the Kingdom of God Realism?* 184.

18. Ibid.

19. Ibid., 184–85.

20. Ibid., 185.

21. Ibid., 186.

22. Ibid.

23. E. Stanley Jones, *Abundant Living* (New York: Abingdon-Cokesbury Press, 1942), 224.

24. Ibid., 187.
25. Ibid.

Chapter 9

1. Roland Allen, *La Expansión Espontánea de la Iglesia*, translated by Adam F. Sosa from the fourth English edition (Buenos Aires: Editorial y Librería La Aurora), 1970.
2. See "The Encyclopedia of World Methodism (Vol. 2, J–Z)," Mocavo, accessed February 2, 2016, http://www.mocavo.com/The -Encyclopedia-of-World-Methodism-Vol-2-J-Z-Volume-2 /311448/843.
3. "Tenemos Esperanza," words by Federico Pagura, music by Homero Perera, in *Cancionero Abierto*, vol. 4 (Buenos Aires: ISEDET, 1979).
4. Ibid., verse 1, as translated by Douglas Ruffle.
5. E. Stanley Jones, *A Song of Ascents*, 44.
6. E. Stanley Jones, *The Divine Yes* (Nashville: Abingdon, 1975), 58.
7. Anne Mathews-Younes, *Living upon the Way: Selected Sermons of E. Stanley Jones on Self Surrender* (n.p.: Lucknow, 2011), 140.
8. E. Stanley Jones, *A Song of Ascents*, 190.
9. Ibid.
10. Ibid.
11. Jones, *Divine Yes*, 58–59.
12. E. Stanley Jones, *Christ at the Round Table* (New York: Abingdon, 1928), 22.
13. Peter Scholtes, "They'll Know We Are Christians by Our Love," lyrics posted on invubu, accessed February 2, 2016, http://www.invubu .com/quotes/songs/show/Peter_Scholtes/They%27ll_Know_We _Are_Christians_By_Our_Love.html.

ABOUT THE AUTHOR

D ouglas Ruffle serves as associate executive director of Path 1, the Division of New Church Starts at Discipleship Ministries of The United Methodist Church. Before accepting this position in 2013, he served as coordinator of congregational development for the Greater New Jersey Annual Conference. Ruffle is author of *Roadmap to Renewal: Rediscovering the Church's Mission,* which has been translated into Spanish (*Hoja de Ruta: La Iglesia Renueva Su Misión*). From 1978 to 1987, he served as a missionary (*obrero fraternal*) in Argentina under the auspices of Global Ministries of The United Methodist Church. While in Argentina, Douglas served as a pastor in the Evangelical Methodist Church of Argentina as well as a chaplain at the Latin American Education Center (Rosario).

Doug holds the bachelor of arts degree from Drew University, a master of divinity degree from Harvard University, a master of theology degree from Princeton Theological Seminary, and a PhD from Drew University. He resides in Nashville, Tennessee, with his wife, Tammie, and enjoys music, baseball, travel, and volunteering at his local church.

CPSIA information can be obtained
at www.ICGtesting.com
Printed in the USA
LVOW13s1251070917
547801LV00007B/153/P